Guys Are Waffles, Girls Are Spaghetti

MI 10/17

PR DEC 2017

"Grasping how our brains are wired explains so much of *why* guys and girls act and think the way we do. No other author dares believe that teens will understand this, and Chad presents it perfectly. This book should be required reading for every teenager."

—SHAUNTI AND JEFF FELDHAHN,
AUTHORS *FOR YOUNG WOMEN ONLY*
AND *FOR YOUNG MEN ONLY*

"When we heard Chad Eastham explain the differences between the way girls and boys think, we begged him to write this book. He has great experience and wonderful insight. With humor and perspective, he helps guys and girls understand themselves and each other better. And that is pretty much life changing."

—MARY GRAHAM,
PRESIDENT OF WOMEN OF FAITH

"Talk about great pairings: PB & J; manicures and pedicures; chocolate and strawberries; waffles and spaghetti; and now Pam, Bill, and Chad!

The combined wisdom, insight, and dynamic communication skills from this trio is a veritable relationship trifecta—a triple dose of understanding. To take the "waffles and spaghetti" message and make it accessible to teens is a stroke of genius—so now young adults can make their way through the haze of hormones and the maze of finding a mate armed with great information about how the different genders are hardwired. Pam, Bill, and Chad creatively communicate truth that is relevant, informs, and transforms."

—ANITA RENFROE,
COMEDIAN, AUTHOR

"Thanks to Chad and this amazing book! I have learned a lot about both guys and myself."

—AMBER,
A TEEN

"I just want to thank you for writing such a meaningful book. It really helped me in the way I view guys, and it really strengthened my relationship with God. Thanks for your insight in this book."

—JESSICA,
A TEEN

"I laughed, I cried, I lost five pounds. This book changed my life. Oh, wait . . . someone else should be writing this . . ."

—CHAD

Guys Are Waffles
Girls Are Spaghetti

Chad Eastham

Bill & Pam Farrel

THOMAS NELSON
Since 1798

NASHVILLE   DALLAS   MEXICO CITY   RIO DE JANEIRO   BEIJING

Published in Nashville, Tennessee, by Thomas Nelson. Thomas Nelson is a registered trademark of Thomas Nelson, Inc.

Page design and illustrations: Walter Petrie

Thomas Nelson, Inc., titles may be purchased in bulk for educational, business, fundraising, or sales promotional use. For information, please e-mail SpecialMarkets@ ThomasNelson.com.

With kind permission of Harvest House Publishers and Bill and Pam Farrel for the use of material from their original work, *Men Are Like Waffles, Women Are Like Spaghetti.*

This story is based, in part, on true events, but certain liberties have been taken with names, places, and dates, and the characters' names have been changed in this story to protect their identification. Therefore, the persons and characters portrayed bear absolutely no resemblance whatever to the persons who were actually involved in the true events described in this book.

Unless otherwise noted, all Scripture verses are taken from The HOLY BIBLE: NEW INTERNATIONAL VERSION®. © 1973, 1978, 1984 by International Bible Society. Used by permission of Zondervan Publishing House. All rights reserved. Scripture quotations marked NLT are from the *Holy Bible*, New Living Translation. © 1996. Used by permission of Tyndale House Publishers, Inc., Wheaton, Illinois 60189. All rights reserved.

Library of Congress Cataloging-in-Publication Data

Eastham, Chad, 1980–
    Guys are waffles, girls are spaghetti / Chad Eastham with Bill and Pam Farrel.
      p. cm.
    Includes bibliographical references (p.).
    ISBN 978-1-4003-1516-1
    1. Teenagers. 2. Interpersonal communication. 3. Interpersonalrelations.
I. Farrel, Bill, 1959– II. Farrel, Pam, 1959– III. Title.
HQ796.E24 2009
248.8'3—dc22   2009021704

Printed in the United States of America

13 14 QG 8 7

Table of Contents

To actual waffles and spaghetti . . .

You are delicious and provide a great analogy.

—Chad

To Brock, Zach, and Caleb . . .
Our wise, discerning sons. God will bless you for
your good, God-honoring choices.

"Those who honor me [God] I will honor . . ."
—1 Samuel 2:30

—Bill and Pam

A Note from Chad

Who are you people anyway?

I, Chad, heard a great analogy in a lecture once that mentioned waffles and spaghetti as girls and guys. When I looked it up, sure enough, there was a collection of books for adults on the subject by Bill and Pam Farrel. I found the analogy worked great with students and eventually the Farrels and I got in touch. We have talked for the last few years about taking this concept and applying it to you, the teenager.

And with Bill and Pam's extensive knowledge on relationships and counseling, and my background in research, writing, and speaking with teens, we finally got this thing cranked out. And we like it. We also noticed that my girl editor, MacKenzie, and I expressed our thoughts and opinions in a very waffle and spaghetti kind of way throughout the book. So we left some comments in just for your entertainment. We hope you like these pages more than we do. It is your book after all . . .

Why Alex Hates Me . . .

I received my first piece of hate mail this past year. To be honest, I was really excited. I mean how often do people go out of their way to sit down and say how much they disapprove of you as a human? I am honored when teens write me to tell me their stories, ask their questions, pass on their jokes, or share some of the random craziness in their lives. But I usually get positive things written to me. I had never received mail that just said, "Hey, dude, I don't even like your existence. I want you to know that I don't like you, and I think you're dumb and ugly . . . so take that." Until this one . . .

It was from a guy named Alex. He had a strong opinion about the first book I wrote:

Hey Man,

I just wanted to write you to tell you some stuff. I think it's cool that apparently you go around talking to kids like us and helping people out and stuff, but I also think that you're full of crap, man, and I just have to say that. I mean . . . you can't just go around saying things like guys are this way and girls are that way like you know what we are and why we do the things we do. You can't just say that people are a certain way when you don't know anything about them and stuff. I just think that's stupid, and you don't know everything, so don't act like it. It's a total scam, man. So no offense or anything, but I think you are wrong and shouldn't say the things you say. So, yeah. I guess that's it.

Bye.

Jackpot! This was a pretty decent hate letter. I mean, he got pretty bold, but he still tried to be polite by saying hello and good-bye in his own special way. He used some good, strong verbs, got his emotions out, and ended the letter kind of awkwardly . . . which happens to be the perfect way for a teenage guy to end a letter. Then I thought about how much I would have sounded like that in high school. (This letter wasn't copied word for word, by the way, but it's pretty close. I had to change the misspelled words so it sounded like English—there were thirty-two, to be exact.)

I wrote Alex back and said thank you. I also told him that when people disagree with me, I try to take it as an opportunity to learn something. And then I asked a question that had been lingering in my mind since I read his letter: "Hey Alex, I want to ask you a question. Please don't take offense. I am just really, really curious about something. Did you actually read the book? Or did you pick it up in passing and read the cover or hear someone else mention something about it? I just would like to know, if you don't mind."

So Alex was honest with me. He had only read the cover. He told me what I had suspected from the start. His girlfriend who had read the book called Alex out on some stuff that he was doing. His girlfriend also took a generalized view of guys and probably said, incorrectly, that *all* guys act that way *all* the time, or something to that extent. Some of it is hard to tell based on Alex's ability to *write and spell real not good like.*

Alex is now my friend. I told him what I actually meant in my book. He took it well, and he now understands that not every single thing I say about guys and girls and their behavior can fully describe the unique qualities we all have. He also took me up on my offer to talk instead of just staying mad and confused. Turns out, hate mail can be kind of cool.

When I was in high school, I hated to be categorized. And yet I did all kinds of things to blend in. You could have categorized me as a heterosexual, suburban-dwelling, movie-quoting, girl-watching, teenage guy. I used to hear people talk about guys and girls and say "guys are this way" and "girls are that way." I dismissed it, even though a lot of these statements described things about me. I rejected the notion that people can be understood that simply, or that we can put people into cookie-cutter boxes of behavior and thinking.

I still reject that notion. But I also think in the midst of your uniqueness you have *general features* that are similar to other people depending on your gender, age, background, and genetics. The simplest feature is a basic fact; if you are a girl you have two X chromosomes. If you are a guy you have an X and a Y chromosome. I had (and still have) a lot of typical, general male traits and behaviors. But, I also have a lot of traits that are uniquely me. Or as I say sarcastically sometimes: "You are unique and special . . . just like everyone else." And while I'm joking, I'm also not . . .

When I talk about what it means to be a guy or a girl, it is only in an attempt to understand *some* of our feelings, thoughts, development, and behavior. What I share will never fully explain you or me. You will not fit neatly and cleanly into any category, but your gender *is* a physical thing. Your body; your brain; your emotions; and the way you approach problems, romance, conversations, and friendship are all affected by whether you are a guy or a girl. I am not telling you something new when I say, "Guys and girls are different." The goal is to look at how we are different and how we are the same. By first doing this, we can learn to understand each other so that something else can happen. We can learn to treat each other well. We can learn to empathize with one another. We can also learn some things about God.

Trust me, when you try to do these things, every one of your relationships will be better, whether it's with the person next to you in math class, your parents, friends, your latest crush, or the person you end up marrying one day.

The Bible says something about this that is simple and profound:

> Wisdom is supreme; therefore get wisdom.
> > Though it cost all you have, get understanding.
>
> —PROVERBS 4:7

The more we understand each other, the better off we all are. Thanks for being curious. I wish you all the best on your journey.

—CHAD

A Note from Bill and Pam

Food Always Helps

It is funny how ideas happen. I (Bill) had been a pastor for a few years, specializing in helping husbands and wives with their relationships. I had read the research about how men and women approach life differently but knew that it was way too technical for most people, so I was looking for a word picture that average people could relate to.

A man called me one day and said, "Bill, can I bring my wife in? I think she is broken."

When they sat down in my office, he looked at her and said, "Go ahead."

At that she began talking and talking and talking. He looked at me, looked at her, then looked back at me and said, "She does this all the time. I think something is wrong."

In a spontaneous moment, I thought, *Guys respond to food, so maybe I can help him with a food picture.* So I said to him, "Think about your wife's conversation like a plate of spaghetti. As soon as she has touched every noodle, she will finish talking."

In response he said, "Okay," leaned into the conversation, and really listened (maybe for the first time). It took a little over an hour but, remarkably, she finished talking.

He frantically turned to me and asked, "What do I do now?"

"Nothing. Just thank her for sharing, and say nothing!"

She leaned back in her chair with a content look on her face and confided, "That was incredible. I can't believe how important I feel to my husband right now. So, what is the guy's side of this?"

I quickly glanced at my watch and told them, "We are out of time today, but we are going to meet in a couple of weeks. I will let you know then."

After they left, I told God, "I have two weeks to come up with something. Please show me what the guy's side looks like."

A few days later, my sons were making toaster waffles for breakfast. As the waffle popped up, I thought, *This just might work.*

I explained to the couple that men are like waffles. Our brains have lots of little compartments. We put one thing in each box and then deal with one box at a time. I told the wife that she had to stay on whatever subject her husband brought up, and she could not change subjects at all. It was hard for her, but she responded to my promptings to stay on subject, and they resolved a problem that had been bugging him for a while.

I left that meeting knowing that this was something that would help a lot of people. My wife, Pam, and I are so thankful for Chad and his ability to make this information interesting and understandable to teens. We'll drop in from time to time when there are things we want to share too. Chad, take it away and run with it!

CHAPTER 1

You Say, "Eww."
I Say, "Awesome!"

What's That Smell? Oh . . . It's Me.

When I was growing up, I spent a lot of my summers at the beach visiting my dad. I loved the sun; seeing my dad, step-mom, and grandparents; and catching up on some surfing. You could say, in fact, that I love surfing. And in my hometown, surfing is a pretty big deal. I'm not as talented at it as I am passionate about it, but I try. In fact, one summer I spent so much time surfing that I kind of lost track of a few other things that I should have been doing.

One of those things was bathing. Every morning I woke up early, grabbed my board, went to the beach all day, and made my way back home in time for dinner. And then one day, before we actually went somewhere nice to eat, my dad came into my room. He always has a cool, calm manner about him, and he kind of looked at me and said, "You should probably take a shower." He said it so plainly that I believed him. He obviously knew something I didn't. Apparently everyone did. It had been twenty-eight days since my last shower. I know because I felt a little proud about it. I also figured I swam in the ocean every day, and that's like nature's bath, right? Most people disagree. I liked the sand and wax and grit in my hair. I liked peeling feet and sunburn. I also liked that I could actually get away with not showering for a month. As I walked to the bathroom, I remember saying to myself with a little grin on my face, "I love being a guy."

> MacKenzie: Just a note from your editor . . . seriously, this is really gross.
>
> Chad: Thank you.

Why It's Great to Be a Guy:

- A trip anywhere, for any amount of time, requires only one bag.
- We can kill our own food without any feelings of guilt for the bunny.
- A guy can dismiss almost any problem, annoyance, or confusing situation with the phrase "Whatever!" followed by walking away—a negative quality, according to females everywhere.
- We get extra credit for even the slightest act of thoughtfulness.
- We can pee standing up anywhere on earth.
- Car mechanics tell us the truth.

- We can sit quietly or play a game with a friend for hours without ever thinking, *He must be mad at me*.
- If someone forgets to tell us something important, he can still be our friend.
- If someone else shows up at a party in the same exact outfit we're wearing, we just found our new BFF.
- None of our buds ever traps us with statements like, "So, notice anything different?"
- No one expects us to know the names of more than five colors.
- We don't have to shave anywhere below the neck.
- A few loud burps and other "noises" are generally expected and tolerated by most people.
- All phone conversations can be done in under thirty seconds.
- Our bathroom lines are 97.8 percent shorter.

Weekends Are for Girls

Annie's weekend turned out pretty awesome, thanks to her natural female flair for fun and creativity. Friday afternoon she finished her report on female inventors of the past century, which included some really cool inventions like the fire escape, life raft, rotary engine, circular saw, Kevlar, and the chocolate chip cookie. Later, all of her friends came over for the first segment in a weekend of endless girl-only fun and relaxation. She and her sister cooked a theme meal for her

girls'-night-in, which featured only Moroccan food. Then they piled in the basement that night with the amazing amount of pillows that only girls can conjure up, watched movies, talked until late in the night, and finally fell asleep with stomach pains from so much laughing.

The next morning Annie and her friends ate a great breakfast and headed out to a nature party in their favorite city park where they met up with a few more girlfriends. They planted trees and made a very eclectic design out of pinecones, leaves, and trimmings, which they left on display as a tribute to the event. Then the girls headed to a spa where they had pedicures and laughed about how guys never enjoy getting pampered like this. Energized, they went to the Cracked Pot, a pottery painting boutique, where they painted pottery to represent their own unique personalities. After dinner and bowling, they headed back to Annie's house for a girls' dance and karaoke party that went on for hours. Later, when Annie and two of her friends sat laughing on the couch, in a quick but insightful moment, her friend Nicole just looked at her and said, "Isn't it great to be girls?!"

One time I (Chad) was not a girl. In fact, I've always not been a girl. But I know some. And there are definitely some benefits to being a girl.

> MacKenzie: Um, this is a little lame. And weird.

> Chad: I know, but when I got up this morning, I was a guy. Still. I have my limits, Mac.

Why It's Great to Be a Girl:

- You can cry without pretending there's something under your contact.
- Speeding ticket? What's that?

- You actually get extra points for watching sports.
- If you're a lousy athlete, you don't necessarily question your worth as a human being.
- You don't feel the need to deny going to the tanning bed.
- You possibly could live your whole life without having to endure a group shower.
- You'll never have to decide where to hide your nose hair clippers.
- If the person you're dating is much better at something than you are, it doesn't kill your ego.
- Talking and people watching can be a great time.
- Your friend won't think you're weird when you ask if there's spinach in your teeth.
- If you're under six-feet tall, you don't have to lie about it.
- You'll never regret piercing your ears.
- You don't have to make awkward adjustments to private parts in public.
- If you have big ears, no one has to know.
- No one can ever say to you, "Stop acting like a girl."

CHAPTER 2

Waffles and Spaghetti

Teenager (n.) [lat **adolescere** = (to) grow] 1. is a transitional stage of physical and mental human development that occurs between childhood and adulthood. This transition involves biological, social, and psychological changes. 2. The time in life where people no longer have cooties; boys and girls act in even stranger ways, and the love bug often hits with all of its enormity and mystery. 3. a time period in which declaring one's independence is of utmost importance while they simultaneously depend on parents for almost everything including food; clothing; a bed; toilet paper; laundry services; and access to iTunes, the Internet, and various texting devices. In other words . . . a very strange and somewhat delusional time in one's life.

It is no secret that girls can find guys utterly confusing:

Chad,

I know that guys don't usually talk as much as girls do, but this isn't about that, it's about listening. My boyfriend, Greg, cares about me, and he actually goes out of his way to spend time with me and stuff, which I really appreciate. But I just don't know why guys are so bad at listening. I am having a hard time with some stuff in my life, you know, usual girl stuff, I guess. Whenever I try to talk to him about things, we always end up arguing. He never listens! He says he is listening, but he just tries to tell me what to do or how to fix my problem. I don't want him to tell me what to do; I just need him there to be my friend and listen when I have issues. Why are guys always trying to fix things and give advice? It's like if he doesn't do that, he doesn't know what to do! Is this normal?

Heidi

It is also not a secret that guys can find girls totally confusing:

Chad,

Hey man, I have a question about my girlfriend. So you know how girls are always complaining about how guys don't listen and stuff? Well, I was trying to listen to my girlfriend when she was upset with her parents and a few of her friends. I actually tried really hard to pay attention. When I told her that maybe she had taken what her friend said the wrong way, she just got mad at me! All I did was try to help and fix the problem, and she got more upset. Basically it doesn't seem like listening worked. And the even stranger part was that she was fine the next day. And nothing happened! Why does she need to vent for hours about stuff if it won't bother her the next day? It seems like she could just skip the big emotional part and be fine. I dunno . . . I don't get it, and I thought maybe you could make sense of this, 'cause I can't.

Will . . . Confused (probably not his last name)

Guys and girls are very different, plain and simple. Sure we have a lot in common; we both like oxygen, food, clothing (girls apparently more than guys), and pictures of baby polar bears. After these similarities, however, you will also find that we are often worlds apart.

If you want to have relationships that add to the quality of your life rather than make you exhausted, sad, frustrated, or hurt, try to understand the opposite sex a little more. Might I suggest thinking about it this way?

Guys are waffles, and girls are spaghetti.

At first this may seem silly, but stay with me. This picture really works, and guys "get it" because it involves food. Even as I write this I have a strange craving for pasta and waffles . . .

Guys Are Waffles

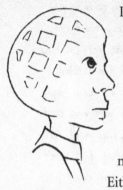

Imagine the shape of a waffle. If you look closely at the waffle, you will notice it is basically a collection of boxes that are separated by walls. The boxes make convenient holding places. This way you can fill up some of the boxes with syrup and watch them ooze over into the other compartments. Or maybe I just love doing that. Either way, this might help illustrate how guys generally process life. Our thinking is divided up into boxes, and each of those boxes has room for one issue and one issue only. Family might go into one box, while girlfriend goes into another, while schoolwork is in yet another, and so on. The typical guy tends to live in one box at a time. When he is playing video games, he is simply playing video games. When he is playing sports or burning ants with a magnifying glass, he is playing sports or intensely focused on killing tiny insects in a terrible and fascinating way. Guys concentrate on one thing at a time. This is why he sometimes looks like he is in a trance and can seemingly ignore everything else going on around him. Psychologists call this "compartmentalizing"—that is, putting life and responsibilities into different compartments.

As a result of this compartmentalizing, guys are problem solvers by nature. They enter a box, size up the situation or the problem, and formulate a way to act on it or solve it. In the sports we guys choose to play, we consider what it will take to be successful, decide how good we might be able to be, and then focus on accomplishing some goals. In communication, guys usually are more concerned with the main point and getting there as quickly as possible. They are not as concerned with talking for lengths of time just to feel closer as they discuss something.

For guys social influence is also incredibly powerful, whether we know it or not. Being influential in a social way builds confidence, and it is attractive to girls. This is one reason guys spend time being the *class clown*, working on their sense of humor, achieving and succeeding in sports, and a thousand other things. This might help explain why guys crack jokes and don't seem to realize that it can hurt someone's feelings. Saying a girl has funny teeth in front of other people will not be funny to the girl, but the guy might be living in the "I'm a funny guy" box and forget about the "girls don't like to be embarrassed in front of everyone in class, you idiot" box. Time in the "apologize" box will be necessary later.

Class clown (n.) 1. The quintessential jokester who is usually a guy and compensating for a lack of stellar looks or ability to diligently do homework; he uses a sense of humor in hopes of scoring big with the ladies. 2. A big, attention-seeking, loud-mouth who will most likely end up in a sales position.

Here is a very important thing to know about guys as far as our waffle boxes go. A guy will strategically organize his life in boxes and then spend most of his time in the boxes where he is successful, where he gets attention, and where he gets affirmed. He will equally ignore the boxes and areas of his life that confuse him, make him feel like a failure, or where he gets little or no reward. Guys will avoid negative boxes like the plague. For instance, a guy named Joe finds out that by being funny, people will look up to him, he gets teased less, and girls seem to giggle and warm up to him more . . . guess what? Joe is likely to spend time being the Funny Guy. If he gets bad grades in math class, unlike his buddy Adam, who gets great grades easily, then Joe will more than likely avoid that area as much as possible. Eleven times out of ten (I'm not great at math either), he will choose to spend time in the "ha ha" box.

Even in categories like laziness, guys think they can succeed. If a guy is bad at his job, or at meeting his parents' expectations and the expectations of other people around him, he may find out that he is pretty good at being lazy. I still have a number of friends who think this is a prestigious club. Girls usually disagree. Still, the guy may develop a commitment to being lazy because he knows he can do that today with the same proficiency as yesterday.

Guys also take this "success" approach to the way they communicate. If they talk to girls, their girlfriends, or other people's parents and get a desirable outcome or affirmation, they will be highly motivated to continue talking with these people. If, on the other hand (this will sound familiar to a lot of girls), the conversation seems pointless or he finds trying to understand the girl he is listening to impossible, he will lose motivation to talk and clam up! This might help shed some light on the moments where guys make very profound comments to girls, such as: "Where are you trying to go with this conversation? Can you just please get to the point?" Or the most common . . . "What?" This word is usually accompanied by a furrowed brow, squinted eyes, and a wrinkled forehead. This means that the male is confused. A guy makes these statements out of frustration. Either he doesn't understand, or he doesn't know how to make the conversation work. For a guy, it's like being in the middle of a hockey game; you are playing hard and following all the rules, but then suddenly the rules change and the puck is gone and the score is measured in smiley faces. And then miniature horses come out onto the ice and start galloping all miniature horse-like! And suddenly all the other players start singing songs in unison and yelling, "We're winning, we're winning!" (I have had nightmares like that.) This is how lost guys can feel when they are trying to follow along with a talkative girl. There isn't a right or a wrong way; we're just very different. We don't under-

> MacKenzie: Are you saying girls remind you of this? Could this be insulting?
>
> Chad: I hope not. I don't mean to offend any miniature horses at all. They are my favorite animal.

stand what is happening, how to fix it, or what the main point is. We don't know how to succeed. And conversations like this can become a source of confusion and frustration.

On the other hand, because of his drive to succeed, when a guy finds something he is good at, it makes him feel great about himself and about his life. Guys tend to be very good at mechanical and spatial activities. This is why we get emotionally attached to building, fixing, and chasing things. Guys take on the things they do well at as part of their identity. This means that as far-fetched as the shoot-giant-guns-from-speeding-cars video game scenarios are, when guys succeed at them, this success transfers to how they perceive themselves. The bottom line is that guys will usually spend most of their time doing what they are best at while attempting to ignore the things that cause them to feel deficient ... or like losers. While girls may have the same tendency to stick to what they are good at, guys will often live by this habit.

Girls Are Spaghetti

In stark contrast to guys' waffle-like approach, girls tend to deal with life as though it were a plate of pasta. If you look at a plate of spaghetti, you will notice that there are a lot of individual noodles and all of the noodles touch one another. If you attempted to follow just one noodle around the plate, you would intersect a lot of other noodles, and you might even switch to another noodle seamlessly without realizing it. This is how girls face life. Every thought, feeling, and issue is connected to every other thought, feeling, and issue in some way.

This is why girls typically are better at multitasking than guys. A girl can talk on the phone, paint her toenails, shop online, dabble with her algebra homework, and picture what her wedding will look like while simultaneously texting and eating. Because all her thoughts, emotions, and convictions are connected, she processes more information and keeps track of more activities taking place.

As a result of this, most girls pursue a life that is connected. Even as I write, I am witnessing this. I'm in a little coffee shop, and sitting next to me are three girls who are very loud. They are moving from one topic to another so quickly that I am about to get a nosebleed from trying to follow them. I'm not meaning to eavesdrop; they are just loud. I can't understand the point of anything they are saying because they are all talking at the same time. How they understand each other, I have no idea. But, magically using girl power, they do.

Because girls have these incomprehensible conversational skills, when it comes to solving problems they have a very different perspective than guys. Girls don't look to solve all problems with simple and fast solutions. Girls, much more than guys, desire to talk things through. This helps them process the situation. Guys usually try to process in their heads by themselves first. Through conversation girls can link together the logical, emotional, relational, and spiritual aspects of an issue. These links come to girls naturally, so a spaghetti conversation is effortless for them.

This Is Where It's Funny

The frustrations often begin for guys and girls during important conversations. The guy is actually trying to listen and understand what the girl is saying. She is talking and processing and making connections, trying to help him understand a pasta plate of information and connect with her. Meanwhile the guy, back in the waffle, is frantically jumping from box to box, trying to keep up.
"Wait, I thought I was in the 'stress of schoolwork' box and suddenly she is in the 'and my hair looks stupid' box on the way to 'my mom and dad are nagging me to get

a job' and 'they don't like me dating so young' boxes, and I don't know how we got here, but I don't understand and I'm scared and my head hurts." His eyes might roll into the back of his head as his brain swells in confusion and this tidal wave of information swallows him up. The funny, or at least ironic, part is that when she is done talking, she feels better and he is completely overwhelmed. If a guy cannot keep up, he might not listen as well, and a common conclusion for the girl is: if the guy is not listening, then he doesn't care.

Welcome to Nothing

You may have suspected that guys have empty spots in their brains, and in fact, we do.

Guys have a box for nothing. Girls have a hard time understanding this. Guys have a hard time understanding how girls cannot understand this. But guys have boxes in their waffle that have absolutely *nothing* in them. When a guy is in his "nothing" box, a girl might see his blank look and relaxed posture and assume that: (a) it's a good time to talk; (b) he doesn't want to talk at all; or (c) he is hiding something he doesn't want her to know about.

For example, "What are you thinking about right now, Tyler?"

"Nothing."

A girl might think that Tyler is not being honest and that he wants to avoid something, but that might not be the case at all. He may just be in his "nothing" box. He is just answering the question the best way he knows how. Simply and directly. Nothing. Really.

I have a "nothing" box, and you know what? I love it there. I spend quite a bit of time there, especially when I need to de-compress, relax, and take a break from stressful things in my life. Guys "park" in these boxes to relax. In this "nothing" box, nothing is wrong, nothing is being denied, and nothing is being hidden. He may need to go there to get back on track.

We also have "almost nothing" boxes too. In these boxes, there may be thoughts about our pasts, a picture in our minds, or an image of something we enjoy, but these thoughts do not necessarily turn into words, nor do they need to. A guy is able to be quite happy and content in these wordless boxes because the memories that he carries in them have a significant meaning to him. A guy in his "almost nothing" box has the same posture as a guy in the "nothing" box, and even if he wanted to describe in words what he was thinking to a girl, he probably couldn't.

This is very hard for girls to understand, mostly because they don't seem to have "nothing" boxes.

Different by Nature, Different by Design

As more and more research accumulates, the differences between guys and girls become increasingly obvious. I think God made us in an unbelievably creative way, and if we try to understand, or at least accept, our differences, we can complement each other harmoniously. We think differently, we feel differently, we talk differently, and we learn differently than each other. And yet when we have healthy relationships with the opposite sex, it makes both people more complete.

As you continue through this book, you will find a lot of good questions, odd sayings, and stories I find funny. I hope that you will be able to laugh along, because one, who hates laughing? And two, developing a good sense of humor is a great way to help break the tension between the sexes. More than this, I hope you will gain some insight into yourself.

As someone else once put it, "One gender is not better than the other. We are *equal* even as we are *different*; advantaged in some ways, disadvantaged in others. And it's not as though we live in different realities. We see the same world. We just, on average, tend to focus on different parts of it. Accepting this helps us to cease trying to make each other more like ourselves."[1]

Chad's Observations of Guys and Girls

- Guys like to hang around girls who lower the stress in their lives. In other words, they like girls who aren't self-centered or too demanding (low-maintenance) and don't bring unnecessary drama.
- Females bring up difficult subjects more often than males because they are more motivated to work things out. After all, not everything can be solved by saying, "Whatever."
- Guys tend to get angry when they are provoked by another person in a competitive game or in an encounter with the opposite sex. Girls tend to get angry when they face a circumstance that seems to be out of their control.
- Girls struggle with depression more often than guys.
- Girls tend to be attracted to guys who demonstrate dominance in their social settings. Guys tend to be

attracted to girls who are physically attractive to them. These are not the traits, however, that remain attractive in long-term relationships. Over time, friendship, conflict resolution, acceptance, and sacrifice become the traits in both sexes that are most attractive.

- Guys and girls experience emotions at about the same rate and intensity, but girls are much better at expressing them. Guys tend to avoid them or stuff them away. When upset, guys typically do something physically active; girls typically express themselves emotionally.

- Girls are more concerned than guys about what others think of them. Guys are more concerned about what they think of themselves. If a guy is confident, he will give himself the benefit of the doubt in just about everything. If he lacks confidence, he will be critical of himself in just about everything.

CHAPTER 3

Chromosomes and Rocket Launchers

A toy company tried to accommodate a suggestion for a dollhouse that boys and girls would both like. However, when testing it, the designers found that little girls played with the dollhouse by moving furniture around, dressing up dolls, and putting them in the house. The little boys, meanwhile, launched the baby carriages off of the dollhouse roof.[1]

Let's Start at the Beginning . . .

Our identities as guys and girls begin first with our biology. Long before you girls put on your first pink dresses, or we boys started pummeling each other on the playground, we became distinctly girl or distinctly boy.

I'll illustrate this in terms of waffles and spaghetti. Both of these items begin with wheat flour but become very different as more ingredients are added and the food gets prepared. In the same way, apart from a DNA test, you cannot tell the sex of an embryo at the beginning of a pregnancy. Sometime during the second month of pregnancy, if there is a Y chromosome, the male developmental process begins. If a Y chromosome is not present, the embryo will continue developing as a female. As a result, the fetal development of a little girl is a much calmer process than that of a little boy. The development of a boy includes a wash of testosterone, growth of a penis, and typically involves more turning and kicking in the womb.

When the signal fires off that there is a Y chromosome present, this specifically impacts the developing gonads, or reproductive glands. Guys will laugh at the word *gonads*. Moving on. In a male, the gonads become the testes, while in a female they become the ovaries. The influence of both the testes and the ovaries impacts all kinds of things during the development of the fetus. These influences include muscle, how your brain develops, hair color, body chemistry, genitalia, liver size, how tall you are, if you get freckles, and all the other differences between the sexes.[2]

Whether or not you are a male or female also determines the levels of hormones and chemicals that are present in your body. Guys have a large amount of testosterone, and girls have a large amount of estrogen. These chemicals have a profound influence on every aspect of our lives. Just ask your parents.

X and Y

The nucleus of every cell in the human body has forty-six chromosomes that determine our physical features. These forty-six chromosomes are made up of twenty-three matched pairs. Every single aspect of your physical makeup—including hair color, eye color, height, and the functioning of your internal organs—is determined by these combinations of chromosomes.

One set of these chromosomes differs from the other twenty-two pairs. In women, the two chromosomes are relatively long and resemble each other. These are called *X chromosomes*. In men, one of the chromosomes is long, but the other is very short.

The short chromosome is referred to as the *Y chromosome*. Simply put, if you have a Y chromosome, you develop as a male; if you do not have a Y chromosome, you develop as a female.

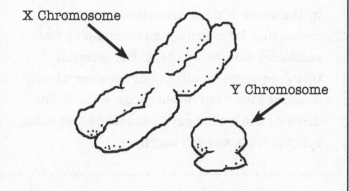

X Chromosome

Y Chromosome

Guys Interrupt

Some of these hormones cause the intense development process in a male embryo. Even before birth, messages bombard him. For the guys, I'll put it in more interesting military terms and use words like *chemical attacks*, *bombings*, and *missile launches*.

An assault team assembles on the little developing baby in the mom's belly and yells out on a loudspeaker, "Stop all development of the female genitals." Another order comes from command central, "Turn on the juice. Fill the armory with *testosterone* and androgens." The first torpedo gets loaded and released at about two months into the tiny guy's development. It explodes upon the boy's world and begins a six-week assault that surrounds him in a testosterone bath (sounds like a cheesy cologne name) and rocks his little baby world. Certain connections between the two sides of his brain are severed, and others are prevented from developing.[3] Ladies, please don't make any jokes about that.

> Testosterone: n. 1. a hormone that is a hydroxy steroid ketone $C19H28O2$ produced especially by the testes or made synthetically and is responsible for inducing and maintaining male secondary sex characters. 2. The chemical that guys blame for all of their behavior when someone says, "You're being a pervert." 3. The driving force behind guys' random desires to hit, punch, tackle, and yell angrily.

Other portions of his brain are sent into hyperdrive. New links called *androgen receptors* are established, allowing the male hormones to freely reach their targets.

At roughly fourteen weeks, the level of testosterone in the male fetus is about as high as it will be during puberty. But then the assault is suddenly called off, and hormone levels drop very low. Later in life, as a young teenager, another assault of testosterone will begin to change the guy's brain and body makeup. This is what we refer to as *puberty*. Basically, guys get taller while having our voices crack pretty badly, which is not awesome at all. And it all happens because of weird things that occurred when we lived in our mom's belly before we were even born.[4]

Volleyball Poets

Some people believe the differences between guys and girls are only because of what our culture teaches us. People call how society teaches guys and girls to behave *sociological influences* on gender. They would say the primary reason we are the way we are is because we have been taught to be that way by our parents, educators, society, and media. Many of the differences can be attributed to the influence of the culture we live in, but the whole truth is much more complicated than that. For example, if it weren't left to genetics, I would have signed up or "learned" how to be six-foot-two instead of barely six feet tall. I would have also signed up to be a genius, a speed reader, a phenomenally great poet, and an exceptional volleyball player while I was at it. But before we get into that, it might be helpful to learn more about some other things that make us unique . . .

Use Your Head

The structure and operation of the brain are fascinating. Seriously. Prepare to be fascinated. The three main parts of the brain are the *cerebrum*, the *cerebellum*, and the *brain stem*. Pretty exciting words, right? Simply stated, the cerebrum is the spongy part, the cerebellum is the control center, and the brain stem is ... the stem. The *cerebrum* (spongy part) is the largest part of the brain and has left and right hemispheres. This sponge is the structure most of us think about when we hear the word *brain*. It is pink and squishy with lots of wrinkles that look like a little pug dog's skin. It's the part that kind of grosses you out, but that you would also be curious to poke just to see what it felt like. The *cerebellum* (control center) is relatively small and is located immediately behind the brain stem. Most brain functions are directed from here. The cerebellum fine-tunes our motor activity and movements so that we don't trip over too many desks. It gives us the ability to write, raise a fork with food on it to our mouths, write our answers on a test, drive, type on a keyboard, and turn the pages of this book. The *brain stem* is located at the lower portion of the brain and connects the brain to the spinal cord. This structure is responsible for basic vital life functions such as breathing, heartbeat, and blood pressure.

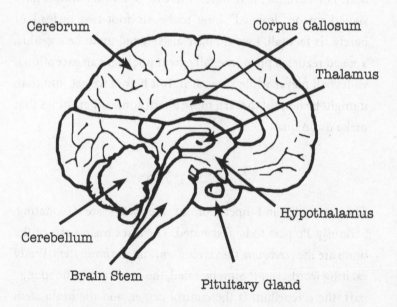

Cerebrum

Corpus Callosum

Thalamus

Hypothalamus

Cerebellum

Brain Stem

Pituitary Gland

The control center has a big job to do, so it has recruited some assistants. The first of these assistants are called the *thalamus*, the *hypothalamus*, and the *pituitary gland*. How exciting is that? These assistants help us function normally. The thalamus gives sensory information to the control center, enabling us to see, hear, and smell. The hypothalamus helps regulate body functions (pretty important, I might add), such as thirst and appetite, as well as sleep, aggression, and sexual behavior. It handles the information from the autonomic nervous system and sends messages over to the pituitary gland. The pituitary gland produces hormones that play a role in growth, development, and other various physiological (physical) variables.

The complex structure of the brain provides limitless possibilities of how the brain can work. The average human brain contains about 10 billion nerve cells called *neurons*. Connecting these nerve cells are things called *synapses*. There are about 10 trillion of those. The sheer number of cells and connections give the brain the potential for an inexhaustible and sophisticated network of connectivity and productivity.[5]

So, a lot of these brain characteristics are the same for both men and women, but here's where things start to get a little different . . .

Brain Structure

The most obvious difference is that, on average, men's brains are approximately 15 percent larger than women's brains.[6] At this point guys might instinctively feel the need to boast and say to themselves, *That's right. I knew it. I knew I had a huge brain. I knew mine was bigger than yours.* At the same time, girls everywhere are rolling their eyes. However . . . the connections in the brain and their organization impact behavior more than the physical size of your brain. Guys' brains might be a little bigger, but girls' brains usually have more connections than guys. Again . . . we are equal . . . just different. Kind of a theme here, people. . . .

Brain Fluid . . . Gross

As I mentioned before, the spongy part of your brain has two sides, and they need to communicate with each other. There is a highway of connections that does this, called the *corpus callosum*. It's kind of like the Internet of your brain; it passes electronic impulses or messages between the two sides of the brain in a gap filled with brain fluid. The corpus callosum and the brain fluid house the neurons between the two sides of your brain. While there is still a lot of study to be done, it is suspected that the components that make up the corpus callosum are proportionally larger in girls than guys.[7] That would mean that the two sides of the brain are connected more efficiently in girls than guys. Sorry, fellas. If it helps, I still think you're smart and very special.

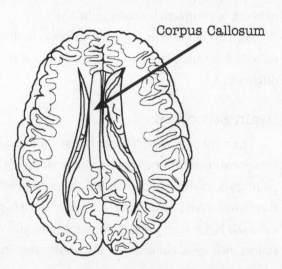

Corpus Callosum

Girl Plan Books

It's possible that because the female's corpus callosum is bigger, generally speaking, girls are able to integrate the issues of their lives together more effectively—and much more often—than guys do. Girls, more than guys, have an innate ability to see the relationships between different areas of their lives and to connect them together. They show this in conversation, planning, and decision making. Rather than separating everything in life into individual components, they can make something whole out of the parts. Girls' brains appear to be better equipped for this type of activity than guys'.

Verbal Skillzz

At the back of the corpus callosum is something called the *splenium*, which holds connections that are related to visual and verbal functioning. Again, because this brain section is bigger for girls, they are typically more skilled at speech at younger ages than boys, and girls tend to use both sides of their brain more readily in casual conversation.[8]

Are You Hungry?

Guys' and girls' brains respond differently to being hungry and full. An interesting study shows some of the differences in the way that guys' and girls' bodies respond to hunger and eating.

- When guys were hungry, they had more activity than girls did in the paralimbic region, a part of the brain that processes emotion.

- When hunger was satisfied, girls had more activity than guys did in the occipital cortex, which means their vision got better.
- When hunger was satisfied, guys had more activity than girls did in an area of the prefrontal cortex, associated with the feelings of satisfaction.[9]

This suggests that guys feel better than girls do when they eat. Or at least that they experience more reward and satisfied feelings when food is in their stomachs. Eating causes activity in the brain that produces satisfying emotions for guys. In this way, hunger causes more emotional reactions in guys much more regularly than it does in girls. The old expression, "The way to a man's heart is through his stomach" makes a little more sense. Although, I do know a couple of girls who could put that statement to the test . . .

Reader of the Map

Guys tend to perform better than girls at tasks that require spatial skills, such as reading a map and finding their way around in a new town or a place that's unfamiliar. While girls tend to use the right, or creative, side of the brain for driving and directions, guys tend to use the left, or logical geometric side. When you apply this, you see that when guys drive they tend to use geometry to "grid" out a map in their mind. Girls will be more likely to use the creative side of their brain and use landmarks for direction, as opposed to geometry. When in a car together, guys break out their mental grid, and girls say things like, "Turn right at that one ugly building next to the grass with the really strange-looking sign." It appears this difference exists because of the different parts of the brain that are being used.

Remember When?

It has also been shown consistently that girls have better memories than guys. Again, this is not always the case. I have a strange memory personally, and I recall details of my life that I have no reason to remember. I remember every membership number I've ever had, almost any phone number of any friend or family member since sixth grade, and a ton of other random information. Also, guys seem to feel good about the amount of movie lines that they have memorized and often feel the need to recite them while watching the movie, even if there are other people in the room. I digress. However, for the most part, girls beat us in the memory category. This also is because of the strong connection between both sides

> Chad: For example, in the ninth grade I learned that the total weight of ants on earth is greater than the total weight of humans . . . which is kind of fascinating and equally disturbing.
>
> MacKenzie: Well, that's definitely random . . .

of their brain—it seems to give them the ability to blend information about a certain event with its emotional impact, making the memory more vivid and thus more memorable. In a positive sense, girls' lives tend to be more vibrant and their ability to recall details far more accurate than guys. Experiences are often richer and last longer for them. In a negative sense, the traumatic events of life live longer also. For example, if you break up with your boyfriend, you are more likely to sit in your room and recall all of the wonderful memories that you had in detail, thus causing you to sit in your room and just cry and cry . . .

Super Woman Memory

Jill Price, a school administrator, is the only woman known to science who is able to remember, and thereby relive, every day of her life since she was fourteen years old. She remembers every sad or happy moment, from the dinners she ate to the news events of the day. Brain scans show that parts of Price's brain are three times the size of those in other females her age. The two magnified areas in Price's brain are the *caudate nuclei*—typically used for memory when forming automatic habits—and a part of the temporal lobe that stores facts, dates, and events. Jill's condition is called *hyperthymestic syndrome*. The first report on the study of her brain was published in 2006.[10]

The Aggressive Male Brain

It is a well-established fact that guys display aggressive behavior more often and for more reasons than girls. A structure in the brain called the *amygdala* plays an important role in this behavior. This structure, about the size of a small nut, is named after the Latin word for almond. (This might lend a different perspective when you hear someone called a "nuthead.") The amygdala is located just off the side of the hypothalamus, and it contributes to behaviors such as aggression, fear-driven behavior, and sexual behavior.[11]

I certainly do not want to go so far as to say that guys have no choice over how aggressive they are, as if we can just blame it on chemistry. Guys can absolutely control what they do. This simply shows the biological influence of some of the ways we are "wired." Life is more complex than that, and we must factor in training, how our parents raise us, personal convictions, and the restraint of maturity and social expectations. And there are certain times in which hormones increase and decrease in girls as well; it's just not as consistent and noticeable as the amount of times guys punch and tackle each other.

Aggression isn't always bad, by the way. When you consider guys' roles throughout history, it might make more sense when you consider that guys have had to be more aggressive while hunting for food. And when a guy is protecting his family, children, or those in danger, his tendency toward aggressive behavior can be a positive thing.

> MacKenzie: I sincerely think this is barbaric . . .
>
> Chad: I agree. Are you saying barbaric is bad? I guess we could encourage more poetry reading instead . . . but I doubt it would draw the same audience.

Punching for Sport

I have made one noticeable and simple observation when it comes to violent things, especially things like mixed martial arts and boxing. While there are

> some girls who seem excited about these sports
> and often watch them, most girls don't. When I, as
> a guy, see these things, I don't mind at all. If two
> guys are punching and kicking each other in an
> attempt to knock the other person out . . . my mind
> just says, *Okay, I totally accept this as reasonable
> entertainment.* Most girl brains don't have that
> particular ability . . . . I think it's because of the
> amygdala.

Anger

Anger is another common emotion guys and girls both experience. Anger signals your body to prepare to fight or fly. For example: If you get approached by two people who are going to mug you, your body reacts. Your body dumps adrenaline and hormones into your bloodstream, your blood pressure increases, your heart rate rises, and your breathing gets faster. All of this gets your body ready to either run like crazy or fight like a champion. Anger is a normal emotional reaction to many experiences of life and can be very healthy. And guys and girls get angry for a lot of the same reasons. For instance, when they feel they have been mistreated, harassed, or threatened, both guys and girls feel the mercury rising. Guys, however, are more likely to experience angry responses when they are in physical or chaotic situations—when a fight is imminent, a project won't cooperate, or they are being directly challenged by another person, for example. Girls, on the other hand, tend to experience anger when they are faced with uncontrollable situations—the car breaks down, a snowstorm hits, chaotic expectations suddenly appear (deadlines or details change), or frustration rises.[12]

Although certain anger can be productive (self-defense, or in response to lies, manipulation, or cruelty), chronic anger that creates stubborn, rigid, and impatient attitudes destroys your relationships and hurts your body in the same way fear does. It is not healthy and leads to more health problems and heart attacks. Those close to you get their feelings hurt more often and lose trust in you. Rather than hang around you and receive abusive treatment, they will start to avoid you. It's like this: If every time you walked by a tree, the tree reached out and punched you in the stomach, you would find a way to avoid that tree. Well . . . it's kind of like that, although trees don't usually have "punchy" reputations.

Guys are not as good at talking about their anger as girls are, and they are more aggressive because of high levels of testosterone. When guys seem to blow up, it's because they held it all in and can't control it anymore; there's too much. It also makes a difference how you release your anger. Guys who find ways to directly express anger, as opposed to letting it build up, are fifty percent less likely to have a stroke than men who express anger by slamming doors, speaking sarcastically, or making nasty comments, according to a Harvard School of Public Health study.[13]

After church on Sunday morning, a young boy suddenly announced to his mother, "Mom, I've decided I'm going to be a minister when I grow up."

"That's okay with us," the mother said, "But what made you decide to be a minister?"

"Well," the boy replied, "I'll have to go to church on Sunday anyway, and I figure it will be more fun to stand up and yell than to sit still and listen."

Rockets or Baby Carriages

Guys' brains are bigger, but girls' brains are more efficient. Guys might do a single task with more efficiency than girls, but girls can do many tasks at once with more efficiency than guys. While you have very similar traits, you also have shockingly different ones. Many of these things will be determined by the people and society around you, while many of the core differences start before you are born. That one little X or Y chromosome can create quite a bit of difference in people. It can influence whether you are more likely to arrange the furniture in a dollhouse while having a good conversation, or if you are going to be busy on the roof, trying to launch a baby carriage off of it.

Comprehending these differences can help make sense out of everyday situations that you will face as guys and girls. It will also help you understand the emotions that you experience.

This will be especially helpful if you ever find yourself saying cuss words in the woods or crying uncontrollably in strange places.

CHAPTER 4

Crying in the Bathroom

Girls. You never know what they're going to think.

—J. D. Salinger

Nicole was having a rough day. Her parents had been arguing the night before, and her dad got mad and yelled at her again for not wanting to watch her little brother. Kyle, the guy she liked, suddenly started sending mixed signals and stopped responding when she tried to talk to him. She wasn't trying to marry the guy, but she really liked him and hoped their relationship was going somewhere. And then this morning she found out that Kyle was interested in other girls, not just her. In fact, she happened to be one of three girls who had been receiving his attention. Her homework overwhelmed her, and she really didn't appreciate the history teacher's cold and methodical relay of the information that was coming up on their next big test. Sitting there in class that day she felt frustrated at her teacher, mad at her parents, fed up with guys, and to top it all off she was having one of those "I feel ugly" days. She asked the teacher if she could go to the bathroom and quietly left class. With her head down, she hurried to the end of the hall. When she got to the girls' room, completely overwhelmed by everything, she shut the door and cried in the bathroom stall.

Sometimes life can be great, and other times it really stinks. Sometimes it is overwhelming, and all you can do is just let it all out. How things affect guys and girls, and the way we "let it all out" is usually very different. While I don't think girls sit in the bathroom crying all the time, it's probably happened to more girls than guys.

Okay, I'm not dumb. You should know that. Just so there isn't any hate mail directed at me, please know that I am not so unintelligent as to actually write as though I *know* what girls want or exactly how they think and act. Please . . . give me a little credit. But there are some things I've learned about girls. As I observe some of these things, I continue to learn. And the more I learn, the more questions I have. That's why I get help from other girls and women. Just thought you should know I'm not a total "know-it-all."

> MacKenzie: I thought you liked hate mail?
>
> Chad: I do, but I don't want to make people mad on purpose. It's just funny when I do it on accident.

Girl brains, as we've discussed, are just more connected than guy brains. That means, for you girls, that when there are a lot of things happening in your life, there are a *lot* of things happening in your life. You cannot separate and compartmentalize everything into simple little boxes and act like they don't affect each other. And unfortunately, you don't seem to have the "nothing" boxes where you can escape for a while. Life and the things in it are all connected. You are a living, breathing, wiry plate of living spaghetti. You are as complicated as you are fascinating. You are both uniquely and wonderfully made.

The Eve Noodle

The garden of Eden was perfect. Adam thought Eve was perfect, and even Eve was pleased with herself. Everything was perfect, and no one was ashamed of their bodies. Adam and Eve were deeply in love, and they spent their days running around a giant organic nudie farm. Let's just say all of this worked then, and their dad was cool with it. And by dad I mean God. Keep it PG, people.

> MacKenzie: Don't you think calling Eden an "organic nudie farm" is just a little bit inappropriate?
>
> Chad: How is that not completely accurate?

Unfortunately, we don't live in Eden anymore. And because Adam and Eve decided their way was better than God's, we no longer experience that kind of perfection on earth. One bad decision and now the world is full of sinful, unhappy, clothes-wearing people. Go figure. Needless to say, the "Eves" of today have a lot of issues that the first Eve never dealt with, at least not while in Eden. You may share many of her traits (both good and bad), but the good news is, you can learn from Eve. And most important, you can know like she did that God loves you and you have a purpose.

Eve Mattered

God created Eve because she was needed. Adam was given the job of caring for the garden, but then God saw that it was not good for him to be alone; he needed a helper. And so God created Eve; she was born with a purpose, and she enjoyed deep companionship with both God and Adam. In the garden, Eve knew her purpose. For Eve, tending the garden was the beautiful making more beauty. One of women's greatest gifts in life is that they bring beauty with them. Don't throw anything at me . . . I'm not saying you should tend a garden. I'm saying that instinctively girls see detail, improve on what's already there, and add their own creativity to a situation to make it even better. Not only do you bring beauty, but you often bring order. Bringing beauty happens to just be one of the many things you do very well.

> MacKenzie: I actually love to garden. I find it very therapeutic.

> Chad: I actually love to throw things. I find that very therapeutic.

Eve Had Skills

Girls can wrap presents better than guys, color coordinate, and do thousands of other things that guys can't do, or honestly would never think to do. Girls just have many unique strengths that guys aren't typically blessed with. Sometimes these things seem somewhat strange to us because we don't usually have these abilities. Sometimes they seem like magic tricks . . .

You Know Mauve Isn't Edible

In one Gallup poll, one of the top three things guys said they appreciated about girls is that they are well organized.[1] You do a lot of things that guys can't do. We complement each other and cover each other's weaknesses. Have you ever seen a party decorated by a guy? It's just horrible. I tried doing this for my friend Jenna last summer, and the place looked worse than if I had just started breaking things, trying to make a mess on purpose. Seriously, it was almost more of an insult than a celebration. Luckily my friend Courtney swept in with banners, color, edible food, and all kinds of ideas that ended up making it great. Girls' brains are much better connected, and so it makes sense that they connect lots of things in a way that makes a situation or event better. Think about clothing. For a lot of guys, it's hard to pick a matching T-shirt and jeans to wear. Girls tend to instinctively understand color schemes, style, and aesthetic appeal infinitely better than most guys. There are several guys I know who think mauve and turquoise are foods. Guys can be grateful that girls are there to add their own creativity and natural ability to bring beauty to life and all the things in it.

You Don't Kill Birds

Bill and Pam did a survey of single guys for several of their books. Hands down, they found that what guys consistently found most attractive about girls related to their relationship skills. They used many different words to describe what attracted them (*kind, tender, empathetic, loving, nurturing, sweet,* and *nice,* to name a few), but all the descriptions fell into one common category: compassion.

Girls demonstrate compassion more readily, whether it's to friends, children, puppies, or almost any other living creature. I really love puppies, by the way. I'm simply saying I've never seen a girl announce to her friends that she has a great idea and it involves shooting pellet guns at birds in the front yard. I cannot say the same thing for most of my close guy friends. My apologies to all birds and bird lovers.

You Can Read Between the Emotional Lines

Because girls are more skilled at expressing emotion, they typically read other's emotions better than most guys. If you're a guy and your mom, sister, wife, or daughter thinks you need to "talk to someone" or that you should "make things right" or asks, "Can you find out what is going on with him or her?" then it is wise to at least consider the request. She might be seeing into the heart or reading a person's body language in a way that guys aren't typically able to do.

You Have Intuition

Chad,

I have a funny, well kind of funny, story for you. It's about guys and girls. My friends and I were over at my friend's house swimming in the summer. A few of the boys got out a bag of fireworks. I immediately had a bad feeling about it. My friend Kaitlin and I just grabbed our towels and went and hung out on the porch instead of staying at the pool. Mike and Phil started letting off fireworks, and then they started throwing them at each other. A couple of bottle rockets practically set their clothes on fire, and Phil's dog kept running after them until they exploded. Then Phil threw some little grenade-looking firework at

Mike, and it didn't go off, so Mike picked it up to throw it back and it went off! He started yelling and screaming. We ended up having to take him to the emergency room and he had some pretty bad burns on his hand. Needless to say, our parents weren't very happy about it, and it took weeks for Mike's hand to get better. Why do boys do stuff like that? I mean, how do they not know that some things are just dumb and dangerous? It seems like girls notice bad ideas a lot quicker than boys do. Well, at least we did! Boys are silly sometimes.

—Jess

Girls sometimes see with their feelings. You girls may say things like, "I'm uncomfortable with this"; "I'm not sure about this"; "I don't have a good feeling about this." Or you may have positive intuition about something: "I feel really great about this opportunity!" "I think we should go for it!" Your intuition can be incredibly powerful as well as useful. Because these are things Waffles don't typically experience, your intuition might be a real lifesaver for us too! This intuition develops more over time. So take it slow, but pay attention. These intuitions often exist for a reason. And they can probably save a few hands from being burned.

Are Girls More Fair?

Even the way guys and girls choose teams in gym class differs. In fact, eighty to ninety percent of children prefer to play with their own sex. Girls prefer girls as playmates, and boys prefer boys as playmates.[2] Even when we do something simple like pick dodgeball teams, our gender influences us. Guys will usually pick members of their team based on ability and show a preference toward athletic males and people who increase the team's potential to win. Girls, generally, will be more "fair and balanced" when picking teams; they take into account personalities, the number of guys and girls, and then the ability to win. While I know plenty of girls who are incredibly competitive, guys tend to be more competitively aggressive.[3] Girls seem to incorporate many qualities and considerations into seemingly simple things, even something as simple as a game of dodgeball.

When Things Are Crazy

Maybe you have cried in the bathroom, and maybe you haven't, but if you're a girl then you will encounter and deal with stress differently than guys. When life brings on stress, that stress goes right to the amygdala, or the emotional center of the brain, and then works differently on girls than guys. When you have stress in your life—boys, schoolwork, family, self-esteem, God,—you react. And when you are a teenager, it is a big reaction. Girls typically respond to stress more strongly and noticeably than guys do. This is, in part, due to the fact that your whole life is connected. Remember the spaghetti thing? As a result, when one thing is wrong in your life, it can feel like everything is wrong in your life. Your mind starts to run, your emotions do flips, and you fight to keep your fears under control. You wonder if the stress is real, or if it just that time of the month. Because your brain produces different amounts of estrogen and progesterone depending on the stage of your menstrual cycle, some weeks you might feel relaxed and low-key, and suddenly the next week be irritable and flustered more easily.[4] Girls also experience more social stress because they tend to feel a higher need to be socially liked and accepted. In contrast, teen guys have a desire to find respect among their peers, so they hang out in boxes where they can succeed rather than worry about being liked. When girls are upset about guys, this social stress skyrockets to a new level. Sometimes it can be hard to understand. While I was writing this paragraph, I got a letter from a girl who was confused about . . . well . . . a lot of stuff.

Chad,

All right, so here's the thing; when I'm around guys, I'm totally myself. I laugh with them at stupid things. I pretty much always wear my hair up. I wear sweats or shorts, and I don't wear that much makeup.

But here's the problem; when I started dating one of these guys, I completely changed. I started looking at all these other girls who are so much prettier; they have really nice clothes and great hair. It makes me feel blahhh. Seriously. Like when my boyfriend looks at me, I look away. When he talks to me, I try not to make eye contact. Because I feel ugly! I know it's stupid. But I can't seem to help it.

He tells me the reason he asked me out was because of my personality, and how laid-back I am compared to all the other girls, and that makes me beautiful.

> But I don't feel that way . . . at all.
>
> And when my boyfriend and I are hanging out, and a really hot girl walks by, and he looks at her, it just tears me up inside. I don't know what to do!
>
> Any advice??
> Christine

As I mentioned, boy stress seems to take things to a different level. Christine's freak-out is partly due to the physical and mental changes that occur when you are a teenager. It frustrates her because she doesn't seem to be able to control some of her feelings.

> **Chad:** I wonder what it's like to "feel fragile." I would probably try it. Do you know how I could do it? When I feel nauseated I think I feel fragile. Does that sound right?
>
> **MacKenzie:** It's a little different, but almost equally miserable . . .

You might understand this. One moment you have great self-confidence, and the next week you're feeling lousy about yourself and very fragile. This is normal. This also causes confusion for the guys in your life, and sometimes, it is *caused* by the guys in your life.

If it seems like you have a lot of extra stress in your life, particularly where a guy is concerned, consider two things:

1. You might need to talk to someone about how you are feeling. (Someone who is not a guy.)
2. You might not be prepared for a relationship.

You probably don't want to hear that, but it may still be true. I rarely ever hear of a girl who regrets *not* having lots of boyfriends when she was fifteen. It's usually the opposite. Girls who are older wish they would have spent less time being consumed with guys and boyfriends and had focused more on other aspects of their lives. This is also a great way to have a little less stress to manage in light of all of the other changes you are experiencing at this time in your life.

These things are normal, so try not to freak out. When you focus on many parts of your life and try to find balance, it helps to manage some of those hard feelings as well. It is also important because you are on a search for something far more significant: your significance.

What a Girl Wants

A kid in a relationship class I was teaching interrupted me one day. He was a little flustered. When we were talking about guy-and-girl relationships, I could tell that he didn't like the complexity. When we talked about things girls wanted from guys, there were lists. When we talked about things guys wanted from girls, there was one short list. Finally, in his utter inability to comprehend what girls want in life, he just yelled, "Dude, I don't get it . . . What in the world do girls *want*, then?"

We weren't just talking about girlfriends and boyfriends. And it brought up a very good question about what is important to guys and girls in life. After all, what does a girl want?

On a recent flight, I read a survey that said what a girl most desires is significance. Similar to the way guys want to succeed, girls want to know their lives count. They want the world to be a better place because they are in it. Emotionally healthy girls instinctively desire to leave the world better than they found it. They want people to be glad they were there.

While this is an incredible trait that girls have, like most things, it can go bad if we look for significance in the wrong places. When Eve stopped finding her significance in God, things fell apart very quickly. Likewise, if you look for your significance in something that can instantly change or be taken away, you're setting yourself up for a fall. A very common example is guys. I could write another book with all the letters I have received from girls telling me how they have placed their significance and worth in guys, only to be messed with, crushed, or have their value quickly taken away. So, um . . . don't do this. Or, if you are doing this . . . then stop. If you place your worth and significance in something that can change—and guys are kind of a given— it's likely that insecurity will set in.

The most unhealthy and unhappy girls place their significance in relationships prematurely. In the right timing, most likely after your teenage years, and over a period of time in a healthy and mature relationship, you will find relationships easier, more enjoyable, and more natural. But God is there before any other relationship. He asks you to find your meaning in him, where he will nurture it, grow it, and never take it from you. You can't ever successfully find your significance in people. It could be your mom, your dad, the world's greatest boyfriend, or even yourself; they're still just people. They will let you down. Guys are there to appreciate and affirm your significance, not create it. I know that's "advicey" . . . but if it helps eliminate a few letters from girls who encounter these things, then it's worth a shot. You are significant because God created you; find your significance in him.

Never Enough

One of our sons is one of those really thoughtful guys. If his girlfriend had a bad day, the next day he'd bring her a flower, a card, or her favorite candy. When she was sad, he'd tell her jokes or give her a hug to cheer her up. How did she repay him? She'd get mad. If she did badly on a test, somehow it was his fault. If she performed poorly in her sport, she'd blame him. Nothing he did was ever enough to make her happy. It started affecting him. He felt hopeless and helpless because of her actions and attitude toward him. He would come home and talk about how much it hurt his feelings that she never said thanks for the flowers, the stuffed animals, the cards, or any of the nice things he did for her.

Pretty soon he realized she needed more help than he could offer (she was depressed and needed professional help). Of course when he told her that he felt she needed more help than he could give, she got angry and lashed out at him. This time, though, he stood his ground and said something like, "You need to talk to your parents. I think you're depressed and that you need real help. I can be your friend, but I can't date you anymore."

He felt like she was drowning in despair, and she was taking him down with her. To help her, he had to get out of the relationship and force her to talk with her parents.

Fortunately, she did cry on her dad's shoulder over the breakup. He saw that our son was seeing things accurately and got her some help. So if you are really sad, don't expect a boyfriend to make things better—that's something only God, your parents, and professionals like doctors and counselors can help with.

When Good Intentions Go Bad

We talked about Eden earlier in this chapter. I'm sure you are aware that we don't live in Eden anymore. Also, there is no Santa Claus. I'm sorry. Things take a bad turn in Genesis chapter 3. Eve eats the forbidden fruit and then gives some to Adam, who also eats it. We refer to this as the first sin, and because of it we now have all kinds of things that God never desired us to have: war, guns, hate crimes, racism, sexual abuse, violent and hate-filled videos for entertainment, and the list goes on. People also wear clothes now. Because Adam and Eve became ashamed of their nakedness, they started wearing fig leaves, which have since become khakis and sweaters. Probably because they itch less.

I don't really get letters, or receive e-mails, or have conversations with girls where they tell me how happy they are with themselves. I wish I did. And it's apparent that the root of this runs deep. In fact the root goes all the way back to that bad fruit tree. When the devil talked to Eve, she took the words to heart, and something went terribly wrong. Eve became discontent. She didn't think she was good enough. She wanted to be better. And in a weak moment, she believed the devil. Generations later, girls still believe the lies; they still think they have to be better, no matter how good they are. Today girls feel inadequate, they compare themselves to other girls, and they have a difficult time simply liking who they are. And ironically, low self-esteem is one of guys' biggest frustrations when it comes to girls today. Guys often say that they hate when girls put themselves down. To guys, that is one of the most unappealing traits a girl could have.

During a discussion about these things, a guy named Brad said, "I hate when girls put themselves down. It feels like a slam to the guy they are with—like he doesn't have good taste being with her."

When Eve ate the apple, she got a new set of eyes—eyes that saw things different from the way God had intended. The first thing she saw was that she was naked, and it made her feel something that had not existed until that very moment . . . shame.

> Then the eyes of both of them were opened, and they realized they were naked; so they sewed fig leaves together and made coverings for themselves.
>
> —Genesis 3: 7

She felt so bad that she covered up her body. And now the world is full of people, especially girls, who struggle with their body image. They see themselves as imperfect and flawed. I wish this weren't the case, but it is overwhelmingly obvious. It happened as soon as Eve tied on those fig leaves, which again, sound very uncomfortable.

This, however, is not what is intended for your life. There is no perfect girl or one single person who has no flaws. The more you can simply learn to get comfortable in the skin that you are in, the more you will like what you see. You may not have everything figured out, but God does, and he hopes that you will trust in him.

Girls

After all, you know what drives guys crazy about girls?

They can't figure them out.

Do you know what guys love about girls?

They can't figure them out.

I will say that for guys, not knowing everything is part of the fun. There are thousands of amazing things about you. Not only not as a girl, but *you* specifically. I hope that you will try to appreciate these things and to focus more on the great things about you than on the imperfections or frustrations. This will result in a much better life, just in case you want some life coaching. After all, it's great to be a girl. I may not know you personally, but Adam liked Eve, and we like you.

Guy Tips on Dealing with Eve

So guys, congratulations on making it through the girl chapter. Are you now an expert on the female gender? No. But this information and a few tips might help your relationships with the fairer sex:

- If you comment on the weather and a girl starts to cry, she's probably not that upset about the forecast. It is probable that a lot is going on in her life, and something sent her to her breaking point. Be supportive, offer to listen, and don't make fun of her for crying.
- If the girls in your life are constantly putting themselves down, kindly but honestly let them know you don't really like it when girls do that. Point out their positive traits, and help them focus on those.
- For girls, things are connected . . . get used to it. When you are interacting with a girl, try to remember that they won't funnel things into neat little boxes of understanding. They are trying to figure themselves out just as much as you are trying to figure them out. When you realize that things are much more of a process than an event, it will help your interactions with all the females in your life.
- Guys, a compliment goes a long way, especially when it's kind and sincere. Girls, like you, can struggle greatly at times with accepting themselves and needing encouragement. Heartfelt compliments, even if small, can go a long way and mean a whole lot. This is also just a good thing to learn to do. People will like you more, and girls will like you a lot more.

CHAPTER 5

Cussing in the Woods

Last night I lay in bed looking up at the stars in the sky and I thought to myself, where in the world is the ceiling?

—A Guy

One time a bunch of my guy friends were *not* doing the following: playing with each other's hair, having a sleepover where we shared our crushes, painting or buffing any nails on our bodies, or sharing our feelings and frustrations about relationships.

What we *were* doing was sitting around the pool in the summer. We were just hanging out like relaxed, slightly bored kids do. And we loved it. As we huddled around a table, relaxing, making jokes, and talking about sports and girls, we were being as typically "guy" as you could get. One of my oddly funny friends, Nick, walked over to our table with a smirk on his face. He looked at all of us and with a big grin asked, "Hey, do you guys want to go spit and say cuss words in the woods?"

He didn't really mean it—I don't think so, anyway. He was just pointing out how dude-ish we were being. And while we didn't go hang out in the woods, it was still a really funny point. Sometimes we still say that to each other when we feel like just hanging out with the guys. Don't take this as advice, by the way. Spitting is considered gross by almost all girls, and cuss words are not recommended. But I will say that as girls are uniquely girls . . . the same is true of guys.

Deep Thoughts

What exactly does it mean to be a guy, anyway? A guy is adventurous and untamed. He may also be shy and humble. He may vary from being the kindest and most giving person, who is willing to give all he has for another, to seeming inconsiderate and strangely disconnected from the feelings and needs of others. He may consistently look for something in life to overcome. When life seems easy, he is bored. When life proves too challenging, he is discouraged. He is capable of remarkable feats of strength and courage. He is equally capable of astonishing feats of laziness and neglect.

Just as we see very female traits even in Eve, we can see male traits in the first guy, Adam.

Some Guy Things
(That Cause Us Problems)

Girls

A very typical guy trait that certainly began with Adam is our appreciation of female beauty. Guys are not deviant for noticing girls—God gave us this inborn appreciation. Before anything impure and frustrating happened in the world, there was just Adam and Eve. Adam probably stared at Eve a lot, and it was all good, pure love. In other words, she never screamed, "Stalker!" or got mad that he followed her around. I'm guessing all of their dates were thoughtful and well planned, I'm sure they included really fresh organic food, and I'd bet no one said dumb things that made the other person cry. Eve never wondered if Adam thought other girls were prettier, and Adam was probably fairly confident that he was the only man in Eve's life. In fact, Eve had all of the attributes and qualities that Adam needed. Overall, this setup must have been a lot easier and healthier than most of today's relationships. Everything hit the fan only after what's called "The Fall of Man." When Adam and Eve ate from the tree of stupid bad fruit, they brought sin into the world. Among numerous other consequences, relationships between men and women suffered greatly, and this healthy appreciation of girls is now often twisted into lust, sexual obsession, perverted addiction, and other bad behavior. And all of these perversions are rooted in things that were designed to be really healthy and good. Lust and sexual obsession should be healthy love, appreciation, value, and protection.

Eve's beauty was pure, as was Adam's admiration. Now guys have physical beauty thrust on them from every direction, and they are persuaded to believe that this is the main quality to admire and pursue. While Adam saw Eve's beauty in all the qualities she possessed, guys are now misled to look at and pursue only the physical aspects of a girl. Sexual addiction is God's design for physical beauty turned upside down, and you can see unhealthy addictions to girls, porn, and sex almost anywhere you look. Instead of seeing love and beauty, guys often just use girls' bodies for their own temporary pleasure. And while this is typically a bigger problem for guys, girls can be guilty of the same thing, whether it's sexual or emotional. We are separated from one another. And instead of learning that guys and girls are designed to complement one another in every way, you see guys and girls who simply take advantage of each other to feel better about themselves. And there are plenty of other areas that become problematic too.

Anger

Instead of seeing guys who demonstrate strength, leadership, kindness, and courage, we often see men display anger, abuse, insecurity, and hatred. When boys live in a world that teaches them to choose unhealthy ways of expressing themselves rather than healthy ways, they often grow up to become men who prefer bad situations and bad habits.

Anger is not usually just anger, by the way. It's a common cover-up feeling. In counseling, as soon as you ask a guy who says he is angry how he feels, the lid comes off. You discover that anger covers up that he feels hurt, neglected, unintelligent, and unloved. There is so much more going on than just anger. When guys don't know how to express their feelings, and don't have anyone to help them process the tough things in life that come up, they often get angry. Anger should be fighting for what is righteous and just. Unfortunately, that is often not the case.

Ego

I can't imagine Adam with a big ego, wanting to street fight people too often. In addition, I doubt that he felt the need to put people down, stick out his chest, and make himself seem superior to Eve or any of the gophers or monkeys. It seems like he would have had his ego under control. He had no need to have one. Before the Fall, he was the ultimate secure man. But today, instead of finding our security in God and knowing that he created us in his image, we look for it in millions of other places. We care that people think we are tough, smart, athletic, and good-looking. Many guys seek constant affirmation from things and people through means of money, sex, power, and influence—but these things will never leave them satisfied or secure. Ego should be healthy confidence, security, and strength, but again, not always the case.

Many things went wrong when Adam and Eve decided to turn away from God, but thankfully there is redemption through Jesus Christ, which is great news. We can be forgiven by him. We can learn from him. We have a new, perfect example of what it means to be a guy. In him, we see all the intended guy traits that were designed by God, and we have the choice to use them as God intended rather than to pervert them. He redefined and affirmed a lot of amazing qualities. He was intelligent, confident, strong, and compassionate. He was also probably more significant to women's rights than any other human in history. He was self-sacrificing, he was great to his friends, and he lived a life of adventure. He was also ridiculously good at fishing.

There are a lot of unique things that make guys great. And

hopefully we will use them to develop habits that are good and loving. I personally believe we can do this and still love to see things explode. So . . . that's good news.

Things Tied to Cats' Tails

It has been a general observation throughout history that guys seek out risk and danger more often than girls. Little boys hit, chase, and create battles with one another on a daily basis. Recently I watched a twelve-year-old boy bait his nineteen-year-old brother into a fight. His older brother is a finely tuned college football player—he's huge, and he's got really big muscles. He works out with other freakishly large college football players. None of this mattered to the twelve-year-old. He walked up to this brother, punched him . . . and then waited to be pummeled. As he was being picked up by his brother, he cried, "Oh no, I'm in trouble now!" But he was laughing the whole time.

Girls often wonder why guys are attracted to risky behavior and dangerous activities. They ask things like, "How come guys are obsessed with violence, blowing things up, and doing dumb things?" To be fair, this isn't all guys. Not all guys desire to see things burn, watch extreme cage fighting, and tie objects to a cat's tail. There are plenty who don't enjoy these things at all. However, overall, guys have a much higher level of testosterone and are therefore much more likely to prefer aggressive behavior than girls. This is displayed from the time they are little boys, and it lasts

> MacKenzie: You really like this testosterone thing, don't you? I think you might like explosions a little too much.

> Chad: If by "too much" you mean exactly enough . . . then yes.

throughout their entire life. Think about it; you don't often find girls hiding behind a barn, trying to make a homemade bomb in an attempt to shoot a cricket a half mile into the sky. (I have creative friends.) Believe it or not, risk is actually built into a man's makeup. We are more likely to get sick, more likely to die younger, and more likely to break bones, usually our own.

While I'm not saying that all guys fantasize about BASE jumping from a dangerous two-thousand-foot-high cliff, soaring over volcanic lava with a homemade parachute, landing on the back of a wild elk while blindfolded and in camouflage body paint, and then wrestling the elk to death with their bare hands . . . while a pretty girl is watching . . . there are a lot of guys who might. Or maybe that's just me. I love anything with lava.

Wimpy Chad

One thing we guys need in our drive to succeed is confidence. As Christopher McCandless, a young man who died in the Alaskan wilderness, once said, "I read somewhere . . . how important it is in life not necessarily to be strong . . . but to feel strong."[1] As a member of the male community, I know firsthand the strange and important transition that takes place in our feelings of confidence that come as we develop physically. Why, you might ask? Because I, like many guys, have often felt pretty wimpy.

High school football isn't a big deal to me anymore. I had

fun, I'm glad I played sports—and I got to put on a lot of gear and hit people. ~~What could be better?~~ At one time, however, it was the epicenter of life. It was also how I learned about physical confidence. I was really nervous about playing my freshman year. I signed up, got the mesh clothes bag and workout shorts, which are apparently a very important mark of the football club, and made my way to the workout room. This could also be called the "super uncomfortable and horribly awkward room" by people who aren't used to it. If you want to observe guys' nervous behavior, you can watch it here. Squat like that guy, right? Sure, no problem. Then someone told me the squat bar goes behind the neck, and I should take off the weights the girls' soccer team was just using and put on some guy weights. *Awesome. This is a lot of fun*, I thought to myself quite often that first year. *I love humiliation*. And when your arm gives out on the weight bench and you drop the bar and weight on your forehead and everyone laughs as blood drips into your eye, well, that's even better.

My sophomore year wasn't much better. Why? Because then I got to be the human dummy bag for the seniors during practice. This hurts, by the way. Our 300-pound lineman and scary freak linebackers would hit me so hard, it was all I could do to just get up off the ground and make it back to the huddle without throwing up all over myself. One time, after one of the seniors punched me in the stomach on the bottom of a pile, I got mad. The next

Chad: I can tell when you have changed something. LOL. I don't think in my lifetime as a human I have ever said, "What could be better?"

MacKenzie: Have you had a lifetime as something other than a human?

play I ran right at the fullback, who was supposed to block me, and dove at him headfirst and hit him with every ounce of my 165-pound body. After that I woke up on the ground with the coach standing over me asking, "You all right? Chad, you awake?" It didn't turn out so well . . . and even worse, I literally gave everything I physically had, and all I got in return was a concussion as the fullback laughed and called me a couple of choice names.

The next year something changed. Within about six months I grew about four inches, and I gained about thirty-five pounds of muscle. I suddenly felt different. When I lifted, I got nods of approval for benching, squatting, or doing something dumb with big plates of weight . . . but doing more of it than another guy. My coach said, "Good job," and guys didn't make fun of me anymore. I walked with a little more confidence, stood a little more upright, and talked a little more instead of just staying quiet. And occasionally, girls would notice I actually had some muscle, so that in itself was motivating. One day, as we started our annual torture treatment of ninety-nine-degree practices, something happened. A lot of football drills feel like public humiliation trials, especially drills that are one-on-one in front of the whole team. One of these is a tackling drill where two guys run at each other like mountain rams in a head-butting contest to see

> MacKenzie: I know I'm being totally girly here, but can we rephrase so that there's no headfirst collisions? I'm all for pummeling people into the ground, but I don't want to encourage helmet-to-helmet combat.

> Chad: I don't want to take hitting out of football. Why? Because it's football, Mac, and football means hitting, which is awesome. LOL. Thank you for your support. And yes, you are being totally girly here.

which of them has the thicker skull and doesn't get brain damage first. I really always hated that drill because I consistently got broken in two. So I ran through the obstacle pads, sidestepped over the red bags like a dumb ballerina running in place, and sprinted down the alley of death into the other human being who was running right at me. I lowered my shoulder, closed my eyes, and said good-bye. Then I looked down. I was still alive, and for some strange reason nothing on my body was pulsing with pain. This was unfamiliar to me. For the first time, I wasn't the guy lying there looking dumb with stars in his eyes and a little snot coming out of his nose. I collided with another large human being, and I was the one left standing.

At that very singular moment, I loved football. I no longer hated physical collisions; I craved them. I started to love lifting, running, and hurling my body at other people. It was a vital confidence-building exercise that made me realize I wasn't a total wimp. I didn't really carry that attitude off the field or anything, and in fact, I was a little nicer to people outside of football because I felt more confident. I felt like I could prove that I was strong when I needed to, and so I established a feeling of strength and confidence that guys look for in a number of ways. Also . . . the cheerleaders made banners and cookies for guys in jerseys who hit each other. Plus I got to put skulls on a helmet and wear shoes with spikes in them. That was all kind of a bonus though . . .

Guys need confidence. Finding things that help us feel confident is a normal and incredibly important transition from being a little boy to becoming a man. I found that confidence in football. Others find it in computers and gadgets. Still others find it in books, video games, music, leadership, or their studies. It is a real need that has always existed. Even if we puff out our chests and act a little odd sometimes, there's a deeper reason underneath. So girls, please try not to laugh at our puffiness.

The Way We Win . . .

You often see guys who are willing to turn anything into a game with a winner. Guys like to win. We like to win at romance, and we like to win at decision making. When we are not the winner, we must recover. If you think about it, when a basketball game ends with a score of 74–73, it is virtually a tie. It means that both teams scored an *almost* identical amount of points. But one team will jump up and down and feel exceptionally proud, while the other walks away with their heads down feeling defeated. Guys show respect for those who beat them in any competitive pursuit. Even when we (the guys) are the spectator, we engage this competitive instinct. A guy feels more like a man when he wins! I can tell you also that a guy feels less like a man when he loses. Like I mentioned, I wasn't always good at football. When I was a human pancake lying on the ground with a foot on my chest and a large guy's elbow bending my nose across the side of my skull . . . I did not exactly feel "manly". It wasn't the picture I wanted in the yearbook. Only waking up as a girl could have made me feel less like a guy.

Guys Who Love Movies

When it comes time to choose a movie, you'll notice that guys and girls often have different tastes . . . to say the least. Guys like dangerous and violent movies! We crave a movie that is filled with great action scenes and ridiculous adventures. We love the testosterone-filled, daring, brave, smooth-talking, and fearless hero. Superman, Batman, Spider-Man, Indiana Jones, Jack Bauer, Chuck Norris, and countless others encompass all that we find exciting. In fact, these characters and topics make up a vast majority of every blockbuster movie or hit show ever made.

> My personal favorite: Did you know giraffes were created when Chuck Norris uppercut a horse?

The movie *300* is a perfect example. You know, the story of King Leonidas and the Spartans, who fight trillions of Persians led by the nineteen-foot-tall, evil-but-kind-of-cool-looking King Xerxes? Every Spartan is a stereotypical tough guy, and King Leonidas is the most extreme; he is the man's man of all men. Great looking and equipped with forty-six-pack abs, he is a walking testosterone missile. He punches danger in the face. All of the guys admire him. He's smooth and confident; he has an extra fist underneath his beard, and he has the prettiest girl in all of Sparta.

There is a reason why these types of movies appeal, on average, much, much more to guys. And it's because guys want to climb tall mountains, meet beautiful women who like us back, conquer the evil villains, and figure out the impossible situation. These characters and stories make sense. There is so little adventure in most guys' everyday lives, largely due to our lack of large ships, submarines, spacecrafts, and the ability to be as smooth with the ladies as we would like to think we are. So we get lost in movies that take us where we cannot go—unless you are fortunate enough to have a submarine. And if you do, I hope we can be friends.

The other reason has to do with that Adam figure. Perhaps there is something more that God created in Adam that appeals to us guys through some of these characters. Like Leonidas, for example. He shows courage, honesty, and compassion, and he seeks freedom and truth. He proves incorruptible and stands up to tyrants who want power and greed. He is also a compassionate husband, a true leader,

> Mackenzie: Do we really need to devote almost five hundred words to guy movies and Leonidas' forty-six-pack abs?
>
> Chad. You're right. We should add another hundred.

and fearless in the face of extreme danger. His character represents many things that God placed in the hearts of all guys. And in every guy is a desire for the things that make us a man among men. I'm not sure if Adam had the Leonidas forty-six-pack . . . but you get the point.

Simply Irresistible

A guy's drive to find an adventure he can succeed at builds an intense desire for simplicity. He longs to focus on one box at a time in his life. Most likely, he wants a manageable schedule and evenly spaced expectations. When it comes to projects, guys like to work on them one at a time. A guy usually climbs in the box and gets immersed in the project. He might forget that anything else is going on in his life, and lose himself in the work. When he can work this way, he finds life to be very satisfying. When the project is over, he will stand back and admire his handiwork. He will probably find the people who mean the most to him and ask them to join him in the admiration. Every comment about the beauty of the finished product increases the sense of accomplishment. My nephew recently did this with an aluminum foil boat/rocket ship that can travel through time and possesses magical powers. I don't know if I have ever seen him smile with accomplishment as much as at the moment he proudly showed us his creation.

But when a guy's feat is not met with praise, every criticism of the process deflates his pride and makes him wonder if it really was worth the effort.

The quickest way to steal motivation from a guy is to make him change focus rapidly. This often confuses girls, because they tend to process life in short bursts. But guys are very different. When a guy has to switch subjects quickly, he gets exhausted and confused. He loses sight of what is most important and has a hard time figuring out what needs to be done next. When he can focus on one or two things, he is very productive; but when he has to focus on many things, he can easily become disoriented or frustrated. He will often get angry or just walk away from what looks like a mess to him.

This drive for simplicity allows guys to sometimes boil down the well-being of their lives to one issue. If this issue is good, life is good. If this issue is bad, life is bad.

I'm a Wild Horse, Man

A guy, at his best, is both refined and wild. He can be intelligent, strong, charming, and polished, even while dreaming of the rugged outdoors. His heart always yearns for something bigger than life, even though he must master the rigors of his daily existence. He always looks to the horizon. He can be relied upon, but he can never be fully tamed.

Or as one of my dork friends usually says, "I'm a wild horse, man. I'm not tame. You can put a few oats in the bin, and I'll come in from time to time for a nibble, but I'm going to run free." It is interesting that he feels this way since most days you can find him not in a big, open field, but at home on the couch . . . usually watching TV or on his laptop, and no oats or horses in sight.

You should also know that guys change. While this chapter talks about some general things that most guys share with one another, it should also mention that you (guy) are a work in progress. You will learn more, change your opinions, and be drawn to different things at different times—different music, different girls, different understandings of God, and different friendships. You will find things you do well and things you do horribly. You will grow confident about things in your life and also be introduced to things that make you incredibly insecure. You will learn what girls like and what they hate, and why those things change from girl to girl and moment to moment. You are heavily shaped by your behavior, choices, and influences. So do your best to make them good. What we put into us comes out, whether good or bad, healthy or unhealthy. We are all on a journey. You may never fully understand a lot of things or people in life, but then again if you did, there wouldn't be much adventure in that.

Girl Tips for Dealing with Adam

Okay ladies, I know our guyish randomness, aggressive behavior, and movie quoting can sometimes be a little frustrating. But remember, we're works in progress. Plus, we're wild and untamed . . . kind of.

- If a guy seems cocky or arrogant, or he's being a jerk, he's usually compensating for a lack of confidence or feelings of success. If you're pretty sure he's not a jerk, offer the occasional encouragement to boost his morale—but not the babying kind; that will make him feel worse. He doesn't need to feel precious; he needs to feel manly.
- If he seems aggressive, competitive, or obsessed with movies where things blow up . . . there's really nothing you can do about this.
- While there are some guy activities that you may find silly (wrestling, punching for fun, being loud . . . among thousands of others), there are often deep reasons why these things happen. During puberty guys are finding their place socially, as well

as their strength, confidence, and voice. Sometimes these juvenile behaviors play an important role in the establishment of these discoveries. Notice I said *sometimes*.

- Guys can experience the same amount of inadequacy, insecurity, and lack of confidence that you can. Even if we act like we don't, we do. If you can remember that guys are emotional and sensitive too, then we'll all be on a better route to treating each other appropriately and with sensitivity.

CHAPTER 6

Excuse Me . . . Did Your Body Just Say Something?

Body Language (n.) 1. The gestures, postures, and facial expressions by which a person displays various physical, mental, or emotional states and communicates nonverbally with others. 2. You know . . . the stuff without words.

Quick Math Equation

Did you know that 55 percent of your communication with the people you already know comes from your body language? (And it accounts for nearly 100 percent of your communication with people you just meet). Another 38 percent comes from your tone, while your actual words make up only 7 percent of your communication. *How* you say things is about thirteen times more important than *what* you say.[1]

You say things all the time, and only a few of those things are said with words. So forget *words* for a little while and think of communication without them. You can learn just as much about yourself, others, and the situations you are in from what is being said by other signals.

Hey Chad,

Can you explain to me why I only attract creepy, weird guys? These guys only seem interested in my body, and it ticks me off. I took your advice that how I see myself is how guys will see me, and I try to live up to that, expecting a good guy to come along. But I only get the creepy ones! ☹ I dress fun and cute, and I'm not ashamed of my body. Girls get mad at me and say I'm flirting and showing off my body, but that's not what I'm trying to do! My friend Josie said I dress slutzy, but I disagree. I'm just not ashamed, and besides, I'm not a slut at all! I just don't get it. What am I doing wrong?

—A sweet girl . . . who doesn't get it

What Are You Saying?

For example, nod your head up and down while saying, "No," to someone. The person will be confused and probably stare at you. That's because you're saying two different things, one with your verbal cue and the other with your behavioral cue. Then look at your good friend, smile, and scream really loudly and angrily: "I really, really like you!" You will notice in less than ten seconds that people are afraid of you.

Let's go back to the sweet girl who doesn't get it. Her situation is very obvious to me right away, and yet she has no clue why she attracts bad guys. Of course, she doesn't mean to, but that still doesn't change the result. It's because she doesn't understand both body language and nonverbal communication. And unless she puts some time into trying to understand them, she will always be very confused. So let's get started.

If you were raised in a healthy, safe home, you will be pretty good at nonverbal communication. If, however, you were not raised in that kind of environment, it will take more work to improve your body language when you talk to strangers or even people you love. Some people get self-absorbed, stressed, or lazy

> **MacKenzie:** Do teens still know what pig Latin is?
>
> **Chad:** Pig Latin is ancient . . . and therefore passed down to all ancestors of the Incas and Floridians who probably invented it. This stuff is super-complicated, but I think they still teach it in most high school woodworking classes. Ound-say ood-gay?

and just slack off or disregard their body's language. Don't do that. The people who seem to succeed in life and with others tend to have body language that says, "You are valuable. You are worth my time and energy." Body language is, after all, the first language. And I think pig Latin is fourth or fifth.

There are several different aspects of body language, and they are all really important to the message you're sending.

Open Body Language

Think about a really great conversation that you had with someone. Odds are that one of the reasons that you had a great conversation is because one or both of you was using open body language. This means there was good eye contact, your legs and arms weren't crossed or folded in an attempt to shrink yourself down, and your palms stayed visible, which displays an interest in the person or in opening up to him or her. Open body language allows good communication, but there is actually a real need for closed body language in some circumstances. Remember the girl at the beginning of the chapter who was frustrated about attracting creepy guys? Well, part of the reason she attracts them is probably because she is using lots of open body language in the wrong situations. At times she may need to display more closed and modest body language so she *doesn't* attract attention. By the way, not attracting the wrong people to you can be as important, and may be more important, than attracting the right people.

When you want to engage in open communication with people who have good intentions, here are some key ingredients to an outgoing and expressive body language that suggests interest in the other person and what he or she is saying:

- Keep your palms open. Keep your hands on the sides of your body; don't hide your hands in your pockets, and don't sit on them. Your hands, that is. Or other people's hands, for that matter.
- Do not fold your arms or clench your fists.
- Don't cover your body with your arms. Don't touch your face, ears, or neck—this shows insecurity and anxiety.
- Turn toward the person. Adjust your whole body to face him. Point your feet toward him; turn your torso face-to-face, so the angle between you and that person is minimal. A slight lean toward someone says that you are interested in what he is saying. A dramatic lean, however, will make him feel that you are trying too hard in the conversation. Plus, it would look really odd.
- Stand upright and tall, and don't slouch. You appear more confident, interested, and assured.
- Get rid of any objects between you and the person. Don't put chairs or kittens or anything else between you and the person you are talking to.
- Smile . . . but not all the time. There is a world of difference between smiling responsively and smiling

all the time. Constant smiling means you are feeling tense or nervous and trying to cover it up. People get nervous when you smile big while they are being serious. Smiling responsively means you feel comfortable and can open up into a smile anytime the conversation calls for it. When people need reassurance, a smile works great. When someone tells a funny story or joke, a smile provides great affirmation and shows you're paying attention. Greeting someone or saying good-bye to him or her is always better when accompanied by a smile.[2]

Shutting the Door

Sometimes you want people to get out of your grille. You need them out of your personal space, and you want them to leave you alone. (Americans actually have the largest areas of "personal space" needs—most of us aren't comfortable with people we're not close to getting within eighteen inches of us on all sides.) There are plenty of times that you want or even need to show you're not interested in someone. When someone gives you unwanted attention (for example, creepy guys), this is what you need to do:

- Don't look the person in the eyes.
- Fold your arms or hide your hands in your pockets.
- Turn your body away from the person.
- Cross your legs and point your feet away from the person.
- Put barriers between you and the person.

- Frown, or don't give much facial expression at all. This will send a strong signal that you are not reciprocating what the person is saying and that you are not affirming it.
- Walk away. Don't explain or make excuses for why. Just walk away.

You want all these motions to be casual and relaxed. For instance, if you dramatically turn your body away from another individual, you draw attention to yourself and beg the other person to respond in some way. Practice putting your hands in your pockets or crossing your arms in a relaxed way. Rehearse casually walking away without making eye contact, without rolling your eyes in disgust, and without dramatically picking up your purse while sighing really loud. It is a great skill to perfect. However, there may be times when you have to make a scene because someone is harassing you or it seems unsafe. If this is the case, then you need to loudly say, "Leave me alone right now." If it comes down to it, confidently and loudly say, "Will someone please help me? This guy won't leave me alone." Try to make eye contact with a few safe people as you say it. And while that may not seem comfortable, it's better than being assaulted or harassed. Sometimes you need to be drastic, as it might be the only way some people get the message. If you are comfortable with closed body language that is casual, you will be very effective when you have to take a more dramatic stand.

Closed body language, when done correctly, sends a clear message to leave you alone. And that is good if you don't want to be around someone or something. In fact some of the happiest and most successful people I know have strong boundaries with their body language. It can seem strange at first, and it might feel rude. But you should know how and when to display interest and a lack of interest. Both skills can be really valuable.

The sweet girl who doesn't have a clue needs to learn to show less interest in people. If a girl seems really open and physically on display, then she will definitely attract more attention from guys. *But* she will attract negative attention. That means she will attract guys who are interested in her apparent openness and in her body. These are not guys you want to attract. In fact, you become a target. I would tell you if these messages were good. I can promise you they are not. If you display your body, then guys will mostly want your body. Remember, guys are interested in buying what they think you are advertising. Not what *you* might think you are advertising, but what *they* think you are advertising. If you want to wear a sign around your neck that says, "Not on Display for You," then make sure your actions and your clothing send that message. Put it this way: just because you have a fishing pole and some bait doesn't mean you want to catch just any kind of fish. People are not fish, but some of them can be really fishy. See what I did there . . . with the fish words?

> MacKenzie: You are so weird.
>
> Chad: Now tell me two things you like about me.
>
> Chad: Mac? Just one, then?
>
> Chad: Mac?

Cute or Creep Magnet?

Are you dressing cute, or are you attracting stalkers? Don't say the second one, please. There is a difference between dressing cute and dressing in a way that draws creepy guys. And there isn't a particular rule book. I don't really care to tell you how to dress or expect that I could anyway. But remember, if the body is on display, guys will want the body. While people everywhere, along with nearly all magazines, might dismiss the idea of modesty and not accenting your legs, breasts, and stomach, you might want to think twice before displaying yourself. You don't have to sit around and concern yourself with all the pervs out there. But you should take into account that you are not immune to the cultural effect on clothing, sexuality, and the messages we send. So make sure that you dress in a way that *you*, and not your body, are what people see first and foremost.

Your Body Doesn't Shut Up

We just talked about body language we can control. But our physical bodies also communicate all kinds of weird things, whether we want them to or not. Some of these things are just interesting and fun to learn about, even though there isn't anything you can do about them. Other things are more under your control.

Smelly Hair

Hair really attracts people. I never really thought about things like this as a teen, but we constantly notice people and learn about them through things like their hair. And the weird thing about hair is that it's dead. But how in the world does your bed-head hair say anything about you to other people? Your dead hair is saying something about your life right now. It's a record of your eating habits, your age, your grooming and hygiene habits, the types of drugs in your body, your geographic location, the kinds of illnesses you have had, and any hormonal changes you have experienced. Weird, huh? Hair grows roughly half an inch per month, so it displays anywhere from a month of information (in guys with real short hair) to facts from many years in your past (in people with long hair). You are basically displaying your health and dietary habits without knowing it.

When I was little, I had really light-blond hair. Then, in about third grade, I got really straight, brown hair. And then when puberty hit, my hair grew a lot thicker. Now I have very thick, slightly fro-ish hair that requires the frizz-control stuff in the girl section of hair care products. This is all simply the hormonal changes in my body being displayed through my hair. If you have an eating disorder, an unhealthy diet, or have been sick a lot, the health of your hair shows it. It will be slightly less colorful and more brittle and unhealthy. It's a natural way of showing on the outside what's happening on the inside of our bodies.

> MacKenzie: LOL. You're such a girl.
>
> Chad: I don't know that you're helping my hair situation.

Your hair also gives off a type of smell called a *pheromone*. Because hair contains little bits of fat that absorb odor, your hair retains the scent that your body is emitting. So . . . here is the strange part you don't realize: When you see a girl stroking, fiddling with, twirling, or constantly shaking her hair around, she is giving off pheromones to people subconsciously. When girls flirt, they do this a lot more, without knowing it. You may think it's just a nervous thing, but you are actually communicating about yourself physically with your hair.[3]

Pheromones

Pheromones were discovered and categorized around 1959, and the term is based on the Greek words *pherein* ("to transport") and *hormone* ("to stimulate"). They are classified as *ectohormones*. These chemical messengers travel outside of the body and result in a direct effect on hormone levels or behavioral change. For example, bees communicate completely through pheromones.[4]

Bees don't know how to talk or high-five over coffee, which makes their method of communicating pretty cool . . . right up until they sting you, and then you don't really care about pheromones anymore.

My Voice Cracked—
How Not Awesome Is That? Very.

Guys, do you remember that really cool time you were talking to a girl and your voice cracked? Yeah, me neither. But when our voices crack, it is another outward display of physical development and sexual maturity. Knowing this, however, never helps when your voice cracks loudly and unexpectedly. This is a pretty strange part of a guy's life, and the odds are that he will just kind of duck his head for a few months, talk a little less, and pray that this strange thing will be over soon. Don't worry, fellas; it will be.

While the larynx might change in size, making a guy's voice crack, some things stay the same. Your eyes are almost the same size when you are born as when you die. And your eyeballs do some pretty interesting stuff.

Love at First Eye Staring Contest

"Look at me when I talk to you!" Every kid has heard this from his or her parent about two million times; it usually occurs when the kid is afraid to look at the parent. In my case, the eyes looking back at me, full of anger, were my cue that I was in trouble for whatever it was I just tried to break or set on fire. For most of my childhood, eye contact was a sign of impending punishment. But it can also be a great way to bond with people.

> MacKenzie: You were spanked a lot as a child, weren't you?
>
> Chad: Thanks for bringing that up. Can you say that again, though, I couldn't hear you through my childhood pain.

Girls who recognize the power of eye contact early are more confident and outgoing with it than girls who do not. Guys, especially teens, do not like eye contact that much. Go ahead, just stare at one, and he will get uncomfortable very quickly. Some studies on this have had people pair up and stare at each other without talking for several minutes straight. Most of the people in these studies reported feeling deeply attracted to the other person after this time. When someone stares at you in a nonthreatening way, your palms sweat and get warmer, your heart rate increases, blood shoots through your lips and cheeks, your skin grows warmer, and your pupils will dilate. You will also produce all kinds of hormones that help people bond with one another. The odds are better that this will be positive if this happens with someone you know.[5]

When you look at people, your face is reacting all over the place. Hundreds of small muscles in the face express emotions that you are experiencing. The other person then recognizes how you may be feeling by how your face changes. If a guy can learn to look more frequently at people while calmly talking with them, then he will be much more successful in communicating with them. He will pick up on more signals, and he will probably find that girls will find him more attractive because he has found a way to actually connect with them.

Eye contact makes all the difference. Your eyes, more than any other part of your body, express what is really going on in your heart. When you are ashamed, you avoid eye contact. When you are embarrassed, you avoid eye contact. When you are upset, you avoid eye contact. On the other hand, you look at people who interest you. You make eye contact when there is trust, appreciation, or fascination with someone. You need to be a little careful, though, because if you just stare at people, you won't have many friends. You stare at people when you are interrogating them, and you stare at people if you lack social skills. The key is to make consistent eye contact. You will want to look away every few seconds and then reengage eye contact. You also want to concentrate at relaxing the muscles around your eyes. If you tense your eye muscles, your forehead will wrinkle.

A wrinkled forehead gives the impression that you disagree with what is being said.[6]

Body Posture

> Chad,
>
> Question for you: Why do guys in my class always spread their whole bodies out all over the desks and chairs? There's this guy who acts like an iguana the way he seems to be lying all over everything all the time. It's like when a guy is just sitting there, he takes up a lot of room. Is he lazy, or is there some other reason? It seems like girls don't do this as much. Explain, please?
>
> —Abbey

Good question, Abbey. Yes, there is a reason guys do this. And while plenty of girls lounge around and make themselves comfortable in a class chair or anywhere else, they don't do it nearly as often or as exaggerated as guys do.

Why Guys Sit Like Lizards

- Crossing your legs or spreading them out farther apart directly relates to where the genitals are. And let's just say that girls need to be less on display physically than guys. Plus, guys don't wear skirts or dresses. Or at least they probably shouldn't. Therefore girls learn at a young age to cross their legs and keep their arms and legs within the confines of the width of their shoulders. This, in turn, takes up less room and probably helps girls have way better posture than guys.

- It is more comfortable for guys to keep their legs apart when they sit.

- Guys are bigger, and their motions are dominated by their larger shoulders, arms, chests, and legs. Plus, guys sweat more than girls and want more air circulation around their bodies.

So here sits Captain Lounge-a-Lot. He throws both arms over as many chairs as he possibly can while he slouches down in his seat, with his legs kicked out and spread out as far as they can possibly go. If you think about it for second, it actually looks pretty strange. After all, are we about to sleep or are we supposed to be sitting in a chair? It's sometimes hard to tell. But are there deeper reasons why our seemingly innocent behavior exists? Turns out . . . yes. Some behavioral doctors believe that it is strictly a way for guys to display their genitals. Other people say there is more of a social reason behind it. If owning lots of land makes you powerful, then the more space you can command with your body makes you powerful too. At least that's a common belief.

And this is probably true, although it's completely a subconscious thing, and the guy is not aware of what he is doing. Guys puff up their chests to show that they have muscle and are therefore physically developed and influential, and they do the same thing with the amount of room that they take up.[7] Some guys might deny it, but our behavior is louder than our words. Unless, of course, they really want to develop bad posture.

Look at Me! Look at Me! Look at Me!

You little flirt . . .

When people want attention, they will do all kinds of things they may not realize they're doing to try to get it. When a guy flirts, in addition to making eye contact, he tends to make other small movements. He actually makes around thirteen slight movements, in order to be noticed by his person of interest, before he even makes a move to talk to the girl. A guy might hook his thumbs through a belt loop, put his thumbs in the corner of his pocket, slide his hand into his back pocket to accentuate the muscles in his arms. He might even put his hand on his friend's shoulder, which also displays his muscles and signifies a socially powerful posture. He may also bite his lip to draw attention to his mouth. He might suddenly start touching his face to draw attention to it. This is called *framing*. This includes rubbing the face, scratching a cheek, touching facial hair, and stroking the chin. While sometimes these are nervous habits, they can also show up when a guy is trying to catch the attention of girls. They are called *automanipulation signals*.[8] And once again guys do these things with almost no conscious awareness that they are doing them. Go ahead: watch, and let me know if you disagree.

Girls do just as many things without realizing it. When a girl is drawing attention to herself, some of her normal behaviors become exaggerated and more frequent. Usually she establishes eye contact more than ten times before talking to someone of interest. She arches her back more to display her breasts, smiles more, and touches her hair more frequently. One of the top traits girls say they value in a guy is a sense of humor.[9] So a guy will often try to be a little more humorous when talking to a girl, and if she is interested, she will laugh louder and more obviously to assure him that he is entertaining her. In addition, an interested girl winks more often, bites her lips, moves her eyebrows, tilts her head, rotates her pelvis, and shows her wrists. She is also likely to get flushed and have a higher heart rate. When this happens, her heart pumps more blood, and her cheeks and lips become more colorful and pink, perhaps showing that she is interested. This is also more noticeable in the blood flow in her veins, including the ones that are on her wrists, which is why she is more likely to display them.

Are you freaked out a little? Don't be. These things are all normal, and people do them all the time without having any idea what they are doing. Here's a simple example: If you agree with someone, you listen more and slightly nod your head up and down to show approval. You don't know that you do this, but you still do it. It's not that different with our natural behavior when it comes to showing interest in people. If you think someone is cute, you will smile more at him or her. It's kind of like that, but with a lot more detail. But the more you notice these things, the more you understand how we are always saying things, even if very few of them are words.[10]

Watch Your Hand There, Pal

Touching is a strange thing. Sometimes it might seem simple, like a high five. Because, after all, who doesn't like a high five? Not this guy. But as simple as human touch might seem, it is not. It almost always has a deeper meaning, whether or not we are aware of it. So . . . watch your hand there, pal.

There is touch to assert authority. For example, when someone slaps someone else on the shoulder, it is usually a way to show their social dominance. You can watch guys do this in groups pretty frequently. Or let's say you work at a video store. If your boss is talking to someone and you walk up to them and put your hand on or lightly tap your boss's shoulder, there is a good chance it will seem slightly odd. There is an even better chance that your boss will feel undermined and disrespected. But, if the boss did it to an employee, no one would think twice. Likewise, if someone is talking to you and then suddenly leans in closer and puts his or her hand on your shoulder, the dynamic changes. Your heart rate goes up, you have to evaluate why that person is touching you, and so on. You may not think about this, but your brain goes wild trying to figure it out.

Sometimes touching is flirting. This is probably not hard to see. When a girl grabs a guy's arm, his heart rate will shoot up, and he will get a rush of adrenaline and endorphins. And you can also notice that they will instantly flex their arm a little. I call it the *insta-flex*. You might have noticed that some girls have figured out that when they flirt with a guy, if they touch him, it seems to get them a more favorable flirting result. It flatters the guy and directs more attention to him. It works the other way around too. Some guys put their arms on a girl's knee, touch her arm, her hair, and lean in closer in an attempt to . . . well, basically let her know they are interested.

Sometimes touch shows sincerity or friendliness. And there are high-contact people who touch everyone. This is usually an obvious trait, and it involves a lot of hugging. Plus, they're just really touchy. There are also those who are not high-contact people . . . they're the ones walking out of their way to avoid the huggers. Some people desire and have no problem with basic physical touch, but other people who are low-contact really shun it. The low-contact people might avoid eye contact, pull their arms away, or simply leave.

Here's the basic misunderstanding: when girls touch guys, they usually mean to convey friendliness; however, guys tend to overperceive the purpose of casual touch. Go figure. They mistake touch for sexual interest much more often than girls do. And since people let their hands run wild, with no awareness of what their body is saying, you get confusing, frustrating, and compromising situations. So basically, watch what your hands are saying, and don't treat seemingly little things lightly.[11]

When Words Have a Secret Language

Have you heard some cheesy pickup lines? The cheese-ball ones don't really work that often. But I definitely know some guys who try them.

- Did it hurt? Did what hurt? When you fell out of heaven, angel?
- Do you have a map? I keep on getting lost in your eyes.
- Hello. I'm a thief, and I'm here to steal your heart.
- Wouldn't we look cute on a wedding cake together? (Just awful.)

And the list goes on. It's pretty horrible. If you are actually thinking of using lines like these, please take my advice and don't talk. But these cheesy lines are not the point. I'm talking about hidden agendas when people are joking around, specifically about sexual things. If you know anyone who uses crude and sexual humor a lot, then you are observing a behavior that has an entirely different purpose below the surface. Guys usually direct this toward girls, but I have seen girls do this to guys as well.

Here is the scenario: A guy starts talking to several people or even just one girl. At some point he cracks a sexual joke, makes a random sexual comment, or asks some sort of question about anything sexual so that people feel the need to respond. This person is using this content as a filter. If there are three girls and a guy, and the guy begins telling sexual jokes or getting perverted, and two girls don't laugh at all but the other one does, then his brain calculates that she is more likely to be sexual sooner, she will have fewer physical boundaries, and basically . . . of the three girls, she becomes the identifiable target. So once again, it's possible that the girl who wrote me at the beginning of the chapter about her frustration that she attracts creepy guys is the one who would laugh. If she flirts a lot, feels the need to listen and go along with any topic they bring up, dresses to display her body, and hangs around older guys who are more assertive and dominant than guys her own age, then the odds are that she has not set up proper verbal boundaries. Therefore she attracts more people who creep her out and don't have her best interest in mind.

Words are powerful, but actions are even more powerful. Make sure that when it comes to what you say and how you say it, you are not nodding your head up and down while your mouth is saying, "No." The more that your mind, mouth, and body say the same thing, the better the outcome will be with strangers, your friends, and all of your relationships.

A Good Language

Keep in mind that your body language should show care for others. If there is one type of body language that will help you throughout your life, it will be the kind that says, "I am listening, and I care about what you have to say." And then you don't have to spend time thinking about stupid pickup lines.

The body has a language. Pay attention.

CHAPTER 7

Talking More Better

The little boat gently drifted across the pond exactly the way a bowling ball wouldn't.

—A BAD BUT FUNNY POEM

Words—The Spaghetti Sauce, Not the Waffle Syrup

So we've covered a lot of differences between guys and girls, but we don't want to miss a huge one. One of the most common questions guys ask about girls is: "Why do girls talk so much?"

It's obvious to most people how often our verbal differences are displayed. Talking is a form of social bonding. Social bonding, by talking, is strongly reinforced by these chemicals in the spaghetti brain. As a teen girl, not only is your verbal output increasing, but so is your need for intimacy through talking and connecting. Studies suggest that girls use roughly two to three times as many words each day as boys do.[1] There is a real reason for this, and it's not because you have to repeat yourself three times for us guys to hear you. Especially in the teenage years, connecting through talking stimulates an area in a girl's brain associated with pleasure. When a girl talks, or shares secrets or discusses things that have romantic implications, that region of the brain is stimulated even more. Girls actually receive and make more neuro-chemicals by communicating than guys do, and these trigger the pleasure and motivation centers of the brain.[2] This means that a girl will like her life more and have more energy when she engages in conversations of all kinds. So now you know that girls don't just talk to talk, they do it for important reasons. Now all the guy has to do is try to follow along and figure out what the girl is saying. No problem! Right.

You should also know that most guys do not have an intense desire for verbal connection (talking), and so, many attempts to verbally connect will be met with disappointing results. If that is not the case, then that's great too, just know that the majority of guys don't bond this way. It doesn't stimulate our brains the way it does yours. If you expect your boyfriend to talk on the phone for a while, you might be in for a surprise. You might find those long, silent moments met with . . . well, more long, silent moments. You might wait for him to say something, but find that he does not have much to say. His brain is just wired differently. Don't worry, you will still find guys who want to talk and communicate. Just realize that we have different amounts of desire for different things. You know, spaghetti needs spaghetti sauce and waffles need syrup, which typically is not words. But, when guys learn to interact with girls and expand their waffle brains, it can be a very good thing. This connecting-through-talking thing is a learned skill for most guys, and guys who learn this will have much better relationships with girls. Because when there is an absence of girls in a guy's life for too long . . . let's just say things can get weird. I'll explain.

Strange Noises in Cabins

High up in the Colorado Rockies in the cloudless skies amid breathtaking views is an amazing summer camp. It has beautiful rivers, lakes, rock faces, llamas, black bears, zip lines, and soccer fields. It also has strange boys. My cabin, cabin nine, was home to a dozen or so campers that had a strange tradition, and I'm pretty sure it was a tradition that has never occurred in a girl's cabin anywhere in the known galaxy. The guys would sit around talking in my cabin each night while a very unique set of "skills" was demonstrated. Jordan was the demonstrator of these "skills." After we showered up for the night and settled down before passing out from altitude depravation and sheer exhaustion, the guys would talk about anything and everything. Here I'd like to point out the first unusual point of this story: Guys were actually talking. A lot. Wait. It gets weirder. Each night during the discussion, Jordan would kneel down on all fours in the middle of the cabin and . . . well . . . this is where it gets really weird. Jordan had an uncanny ability to take air into certain parts of his body that most people can't, and don't want to. With this special skill he could pass as much gas as he wanted and distribute the sound, speed, tone, and pitch for disturbing amounts of time. And the rest of the guys thought it was his best quality. He would kneel there and make funny faces and basically fart on cue for thirty minutes to an hour. He would let out a high-pitched one when he agreed with a statement, and a low-pitched one when he disagreed. It was not only funny and entertaining to all of them; it was outright awesome. This became so normal each night that they almost didn't realize that there was anything odd about it. They didn't think twice about the farting guy on all fours in the middle of the room as they shared some of their best stories and deepest feelings. One night Adrian, one of the guys, was talking about a girl he liked, and Jordan was trying to actually sound out her name with the noises from his trunk region. As I sat there in my bunk wishing Jordan hadn't discovered this skill, I found myself saying out loud to myself . . . "Wow, guys and girls really do communicate differently."

> MacKenzie: So, last time I was in charge of a cabin full of girls, I'm pretty sure we sat in a circle and shared prayer requests. And then we played with makeup . . .

> Chad: How do those two things go together? I'll bet your cabin smelled better.

When Words Get Weird

Funny Essay Lines

1. Her face was a perfect oval, like a circle that had its two sides gently compressed by a Thigh Master.

2. His thoughts tumbled in his head, making and breaking alliances like underpants in a dryer without Cling Free.

3. The little boat gently drifted across the pond exactly the way a bowling ball wouldn't.

4. He spoke with the wisdom that can only come from experience, like a guy who went blind because he looked at a solar eclipse without one of those boxes with a pinhole in it and now goes

around the country speaking at high schools about the dangers of looking at a solar eclipse without one of those boxes with a pinhole in it.

5. She had a deep, throaty, genuine laugh, like that sound a dog makes just before it throws up.

6. Her vocabulary was as bad as, like, whatever.

7. He was as tall as a six-foot-three-inch tree.

8. John and Mary had never met. They were like two hummingbirds who had also never met.

9. He was as lame as a duck. Not the metaphorical lame duck, either, but a real duck that was actually lame, maybe from stepping on a land mine or something.[3]

From Words to Conversation

When it comes to conversation, guys take a more narrow approach than girls. Guys like to know where the conversation is going. We don't want to control the conversation as much as we want to succeed at it. As soon as we recognize something we can talk intelligently about, we want to jump in before the subject

> MacKenzie: I typically like to control the conversation. It's a bad habit.
>
> Chad: Well, I think sometimes a conversation needs to be steered, and then maybe it's just giving direction to things. It's not always bad.

changes. The subject matter in conversations with guys is much less likely to stray into five different subjects. For example: sports. Guys can talk intelligently about sports, debate sports, and have in-depth conversations about sports because of its logical pattern.

Guys tend to do much better in conversations with girls when they have a clear focus for the conversation. And even if the conversation doesn't have a clear focus, as long as the girl says it does not have a clear focus, guys have a clear focus that this conversation will have no clear focus. When I started writing books, I didn't have a wife. Now I do. So I can tell you some new things I have learned about girls. Sometimes Laura (my wife) just needs to get stuff out. Sometimes she will just sit down and start talking. For the longest time, I couldn't make any sense of it. She would start out by saying how her day was, and then share all the things she did in her day, in complete detail. Then she would suddenly vent about some things that were stressful, including people in high school; after that she'd talk about how her eating habits and desires for certain foods came and went, and within five minutes she would be talking about her childhood, what her parents used to do, and why what someone else did reminded her of that. Then she'd end up talking about our plans four months away, and why we should start figuring it out now. As a guy who actually cared, I made the mistake of trying to logically follow this line of reasoning and pay attention to everything. Remember the picture of a guy jumping frantically from box to box, trying to follow along? I didn't know that she just needed to get stuff out and that she would feel better after she did so. I was trying to find a solution to things that needed no solution. This is like trying to find oxygen in space.

What is helpful is if Laura says simple, magical sentences to my guy brain, like . . . "I just need to talk," "I just need to vent," or "I just need you to listen." Wham! Totally easy! I go to the waffle compartment of my head that is the "Just listen and let her know that you are listening, and there is no need to think you have to *do* anything for her" box, and suddenly it's all good. As guys we know how to succeed. We just need to listen. Girls seem to understand this with other girls. Guys are usually a step behind. But if a girl gives them a little notice or some direction to what they are saying, the guy can then feel stress free, be a good listener, enjoy the experience more, and know exactly how he can be beneficial.

Or as I have heard some girls say, "If I'm in the mud, I don't want you to pull me out of the mud pit, I want you sit beside me in it." If that analogy helps any guys who like mud and dirt as much as I do, there you go. You're welcome.

When Words Go Bad
Let's Talk about Texting . . . and Sexting

Communicating through digital means is fascinating. So is one of its most popular forms: texting. It is also probably the sole reason why teenagers and children everywhere are becoming illiterate (that means you can't read or write or spell) seemingly overnight. It is a simple, helpful, and quick technological innovation. It has lots of benefits for quick and easy communication. It also throws a huge wrench in the understanding of what in the world other people are *actually* saying.

Have you ever been confused by a text message? Keep in mind that digital stuff is 100 percent text or words. Communicating as a whole has very little to do with words when you consider all of the nonverbals we mentioned earlier, along with tone, pitch, rate of speech, and other non-text related things. How many times does a trimmed-down message fall short of what someone else is actually trying to say? It happens constantly. There are simple reasons why instant messages, texts, and other forms of the latest craze are so addicting and sometimes become problems. Don't worry, I'm not going to completely be the old guy telling you that texting is just awful, and it's not like when I had to send messages in the snow with no shoes . . . uphill . . . both ways. I text plenty, and it's a quick and easy way to communicate simple things, like meeting times or the names of stuff or funny comments that don't merit a phone call. If you need to know what time to be at your friend's house, send a text. But it doesn't replace other ways of communicating. Or at least, it does it poorly. If you need to know why a friend is upset, give them a call. I know that texting seems to be the norm, but you can never adequately discuss things this way. When people need to express emotions and work through real issues, pick a real way that you can do this meaningfully. It doesn't happen on a keypad. There just aren't enough buttons.

Sexting

This, as your clever mind can figure out, is being sexually suggestive via cell phones and computers. The disturbing part is how often it is being done and that people don't realize they are putting themselves at risk. Roughly 39 percent of all teens have sent or posted sexually suggestive messages. And 11 percent of young teens (thirteen to sixteen years old) and 20 percent of all teenagers have sent nude or semi-nude photos or video of themselves to people.[4]

If you do this, then YOU JUST DON'T GET IT!

It is permanent. It is a terrible idea, and it is never a private thing like you think it will be. There are lots of Web sites where people can post pictures of friends, girlfriends, and ex-girlfriends that are suggestive, nude, or semi-nude just to put them out there. I hate even knowing that! I wish things like this had not even been thought up, but they have been, and they serve as a simple warning: Just don't sext. It makes relationships, romance, and people cheap and easy, and you are not meant to be either. Make sure there is absolutely nothing you write, say, or photograph that you wouldn't be comfortable with your mom and dad seeing.

Some people won't like that idea at all. But you know what you will like even less? You're texts or pictures on the Internet. Cut out the sexting. There is no sex in text.

How to Use Words Wrong

I love you is a phrase of three profound words that brings both incredible joy and utter confusion to people everywhere, especially teens. Some people use it a lot, and others wait until they are married to say it. Most people fall somewhere in between these two extremes. Many people, particularly teens, use this word to describe a specific emotional feeling. It gets used when people feel close, become physical with one another, or become infatuated with the idea of someone they are dating. Emotions are definitely a part of love, but there is a lot more to it. If you think of love only as a feeling, there's a good chance that you are going to end up confused and hurt. If, however, you express love through actions as well as emotions, you have a good chance at healthy relationships. You cannot proclaim one thing with your words and do another with your actions. If you do, things like this happen. . . .

Chad,

    I really need advice . . . . me and my boyfriend have been going out for a long time, and this week he dumped me! It hurt me sooo much! I asked him why, and he just won't tell me! He hates me sooo much, and I don't know why! Plus, he's been a jerk: he avoided me three times and hid from me twice. I had told him that I loved him, and he said he loved me, but this doesn't feel like love at all. It just hurts. Please help me.

Tiffany

You can clearly hear Tiffany's confusion. And girls are not the only ones who experience this confusion; guys do too.

Chad,

    Why would a girl say, "I love you," but then be a huge flirt? We've been dating for a few months and I really have pretty strong feelings for her, and I told her I loved her. I've never said that to anyone, and she said the same thing. But she flirts with a lot of guys; it makes me really angry, and then I get confused. I don't think I can date a girl like that, but I really want to date her. Why would a girl say she loved someone but then not act like it at all? Thanks, man.

Jonathan

When love is spoken but not shown, it breaks relationships down instead of building them up. What if people stopped using the word *love* as a feeling and started thinking of love as a verb? If someone punches me and says, "I love you," there is a pretty good chance that I am not going to believe that person. Yet all the time people say hurtful things, treat each other badly, and disrespect the hearts of others, even while saying, "I love you." This leaves love with a bad reputation. My suggestion is that you regularly ask yourself, "Is this person showing me love?" before you simply associate this word with feelings. Do people in your life show one another love, or do they just say it? If you pay attention, it's really obvious. The heart of love is respect, and if people cannot respect others, then they cannot love them.

Consider love first as an action and second as a feeling, and there is a good chance you can avoid a lot of things disguised as love—it's much more than just a word.

Translator Machine	
What She Really Means	
If She Says . . .	**She Means . . .**
We need . . .	I want . . .
It's your decision.	The correct decision should be obvious by now.

I'll be ready in a few minutes.	Find a hobby for the next hour, buddy boy.
You smell like a boy.	You smell.
How many kids do you want one day?	Answer at your own discretion.
I really, really like you.	We are now Defining the Relationship (DTR) talking.
Do you like this outfit?	(Tricky: This sounds like a multiple choice question. It is not.)

What He Really Means

If He Says ...	He Means ...
I'm sleepy.	I'm in need of sleep.
I do love you, and that's why I want to do this.	I want sex, and I'll say whatever you need to hear in order to get that.
What's wrong? (first time)	I don't understand what is wrong, but I feel emotion coming on ...
What's wrong? (second time, after first "Nothing" response)	What self-inflicted psychological trauma are you going through now?
What's wrong? (third time)	Somebody please help me!

Inside-Out Communication

What does your communication style have to do with your ability to relate to others? Well, almost everything.

- If you are judgmental, your communication will be harsh and critical.
- If you are compassionate, your communication will be filled with a lot of understanding.
- If you become a manipulator, what you say will be motivated by an ulterior motive and completely lack sincerity. People are not stupid; they pick up on this.
- If you are heart centered, what you express will be shared with care for the other person's feelings.
- If you are insecure, you will put the other person down just to puff yourself up.

What is on the inside can't help but come out on the outside. So if you find yourself communicating in a way that is confusing, frustrating, hurtful, or negative to others, maybe it's time to do a gut check and take inventory. It's pretty healthy, and people will appreciate your effort.

Talking Tips

People aren't born with an incredible ability to communicate. They have to learn, and they have to put what they learn into practice. Here are a couple of tips:

Don't Threaten Guys

While girls probably aren't trying to threaten guys, guys might feel that way at times. Many females, including girlfriends and moms, use female-based body language in their communication with guys. Because girls are better with eye contact and have a closer talking proximity, this can include telling us to look at you, then standing very close, with your shoulders facing our shoulders. While this is a comfortable way for girls to communicate, for guys, it is the exact opposite. It feels awkward and often will just make them want to shut down.

Guys open up slowly, so instead, sit side by side somewhere. Play a video game, go for a drive, or talk while walking the dog, but don't always approach us face-to-face, with lots of direct eye contact for prolonged periods of time. Unless we are in the "open up" box, this feels confrontational. Find a relaxed setting—not a bedroom—and don't force topics too quickly. Try to find some common ground that the guy finds more comfortable to talk about first.

Try to pick one topic and stick to it. Remember, guys are not good at connecting all the noodles seamlessly and effortlessly. If you're going to switch topics, warn him. For example, "Okay here's something else that I've been thinking about . . . " He will be able to follow more easily.

Here are a few tips to help you talk *more better* with members of the opposite sex:

Listen!

Developing good listening skills takes time for most people, but it's essential for both guys and girls. Instead of quickly responding, answering, or interjecting when the other person isn't even done talking . . . consider a few of these techniques:

- **Refrain** from feeling like you have to say as much as someone else. Just say to yourself, *I'm in listening mode*. Try to say less and make the other person the center of attention.

- **Rephrase** what has been said: "So what you're saying is . . . " or something that shows you are trying to understand. Don't be cheesy about it though; it sounds weird.

- **Regroup**: Ask for clarification, or ask whether what you heard is close to what he or she said. A common phrase I use is, "Am I hearing you correctly that . . . " or "Is this what you meant?"

- **Explore**: Sorry I couldn't find another R word. But sometimes it's good to ask yourself, "Why is this person wanting to communicate about this?" Don't get all detective-like here and over-analyze every conversation you have ever had. Just take time to recognize what the conversation is really about. I am amazed at how many times good conversations end up tense and confusing because everyone got offtrack. Keep in mind the possible reasons people will talk to you:

  - They like you and want to share stuff with you.
  - They are confused about something, and they are hoping it will get clearer after talking.
  - They feel upset (with you or someone else) and they want to clear the air.
  - They are nervous.

- They have a decision they have to make.
- They want attention.
- They think it is fun.
- They want to practice. A lot of people
  are painfully aware that they are bad with
  conversation. Some of these people actually
  want to work on learning to talk to people.
- They are afraid to let you talk because they
  don't want to be judged or evaluated.
- They have had a great day, and they want to tell
  someone.

And the list goes on . . .

I think you can see that you will have better interactions if you figure out what the conversation is all about rather than forcing it to be something it is not.

Hey There, Captain Encouragement

It would be a bad nickname, but both guys and girls need encouragement. We both need to hear positive things, nice things, and nonsarcastic things from other people. And while some people need this more than others, we all still need it. While girls tend to report needing what's called "verbal affirmation" more than guys, everybody needs this positive reinforcement. And, FYI, one nice thing you say doesn't erase the last three negative things you shot out at someone else. People tend to have a better memory for negative comments than for good things others say. A fascinating study came out of the University of Washington that concluded that happy marriages have five positive interactions for every negative one.[5] I know marriage is not a part of your teen life, but now is good time to develop a habit that you will be glad you have later on. While five positive interactions for each negative doesn't sound equally balanced, it is emotionally proportional. Try it and see what happens; everyone needs encouragement. Wow, did I mention I love the fact that you are such a good reader? It makes me feel pretty important that you would take time to do that. And you look great today! You handsome guy/pretty girl.

Sorry, just trying to make my point.

It Can Work—Really!

I was hanging out with a youth group, which I do pretty often, and something pretty cool happened. We were sitting around talking about a few different things relevant to both guys and girls, when I noticed something had happened. The guys and girls were both starting to engage with the same interest and focus. Once we had gotten into an interesting discussion about dating and started sharing opinions on the subject, the floodgates opened, and conversation started pouring out of both genders. The guys and girls were interjecting enthusiastically; the guys weren't just trying to make fun of each other, and they were talking at the same rate of speed as the girls, openly asking the same types of questions without sarcasm. The girls were waiting to hear what others had to say and then responding with relevant comments. They were unknowingly showing an intense level of interest in a subject. The guys and girls were talking, and they really heard each other. They had momentarily unified and had no idea this had happened. I wish this weren't as rare as it sometimes seems to be. But perhaps the more we learn and the more we practice, the more often we can talk to each other clearly. And it's really important . . . especially when it comes to that dating thing.

CHAPTER 8

Wanna Hold Hands?

Welcome to the world of dating. When discussing relationships with the opposite sex, this is sort of an important topic. Dating is great, but it also stinks. It can be full of blissful, hand-holding, romantic moments, and also lots of fighting, crying, and cruelty. Dating can seem like heaven one moment, and within one hour seem like hell. Some days it creates some of the greatest feelings on earth, and the next day it can be more frustrating than anything you can imagine. Like I said . . . welcome.

Dating: Great Idea or Horrible Idea?

Opinions about dating vary greatly and are spread quite far apart. Some people view dating as a great way to get to know others and to have fun while you are young. Other people use dating to manipulate others to get their own needs met. Some think dating is something you have to do starting from the age of twelve. Another large handful thinks you shouldn't date until you're ready to get married. So what is dating, and what's the point of it? For starters, let's say this about dating: it is essentially getting to know someone over an extended amount of time to determine if a romantic relationship is something worth pursuing.

Let me also say this: dating is a good thing, if you keep it in perspective. It all depends on how you do it. So let's start with a big statistic. About 96 percent of high school relationships will not last.[1] How's that for dropping a bomb? I can tell you, in other words, that it is almost a complete fact that if you are currently in high school and dating someone, you will not end up marrying the person you are dating. Have you ever thought about that? It seems like it's a negative statement, but it's actually a good thing! Too many times teenagers enter a romantic relationship thinking it is going to last forever. They make commitments to each other and invest enormous amounts of emotional energy on the relationship. When it doesn't last, they are devastated. It doesn't have to be that way. You can make dating a good thing that helps you become a better person without ripping up your heart. It means that if you redefine dating more as a friendship and keep it in perspective, you will have better relationships. The average age of marriage is 26.2 in the United States, and it's continuing to increase. The less mature people are when they get married, the more likely they are to get divorced.[2] You are still developing and will continue to change in the things you like and need in a person. Plus, ladies, the teenage guy is *not* thinking about marriage. Really . . . he isn't. Trust me.

So let's consider the big, ugly 96 percent statistic that I just gave you. If I were to tell you that you will date someone but that you probably won't marry that person, then what would you do differently? Most girls quickly say they would be less likely to be sexual with their boyfriend. People who put emotional and physical boundaries in place have much better dating experiences. So . . . date lightly. I don't mean take dating lightly. You should take it seriously, but you should also recognize that it is a learning experience. Think of dating as a way to learn the things that you really like in the opposite sex, as well as the things you don't like; think of it as a way to develop important friend-ships and to offer care and concern for another person. Dating also exists so that you can discover the kind of person you even-tually want to marry and to learn to be the kind of person that you need to be for your future husband or wife. Here are a few thoughts and tips for you to keep in mind, should you choose to enter the world of dating in the near future.

How You Start Is How You End

I was in a bridge-building competition for my wood shop class once. When we were finished, there was a demonstration to see which bridge could hold the most weight. Mine did not win. It failed completely. In fact, it first-place failed. It looked good, I thought. But it couldn't stand up to the test it was built for. Literally. It was flat-out embarrassing. The winning bridge held forty-five pounds, and mine held three. Seriously . . . it was bad. The reason was simple. I was in a hurry, and the first supports I put in were done quickly and not well. Since it looked like a bridge, I didn't go back and fix the weak parts of my project. I tried to take shortcuts, and in the end it showed. Our relation-ships are the same way. How you start them is a pretty good indicator of how they will end.

If people start dating carelessly, they will get disaster in return. It's like putting a quarter in a candy machine, and instead of giving you candy, the machine punches you in the stomach. Well, it's kind of like that.

Here's the point: if two people really care about each other, treat each other with kindness, start a relationship in friendship, and try to learn to communicate better, dating will work for them. If the relationship holds together for a long time, it will be fun, healthy, and encouraging. Even if the relationship ends (and odds are it will . . . sorry), they will end up on better terms with each other and become two people who can laugh at the fact that they once dated. if one of those people is you, then you will come out looking more like the kind of quality person that other people of great quality will appreciate. And you will protect yourself and others in the long run. Oh yeah, and you will learn really valuable relationship skills.

> MacKenzie: I don't know that it would be safe to eat cookies sent from strangers. FYI.
>
> Chad: I'll take my chances. Cookies are a good gamble.

Start well. You'll thank me later, and then you can send me cookies.

Don't Steal My Lunch Money

You know what bothered me the most about the bully in school who took people's lunch money or Fruit Roll-Ups? It's that there were people who thought that just because of their existence, they deserved things. How does anyone ever get to the point that they can say to someone, "Hey, you need to give me your money and your dignity"? Seriously, it's a very strange concept, and yet people do it all the time in relationships—and when they're dating. They don't usually expect lunch money, but they do feel that people owe them something.

Some girls demand all of their boyfriends' attention, time,

compliments, and emotions. Teen guys are not ready for deep emotional commitment. Forcing this upon them in any way creates a really strange, hurtful cycle in your life. At first, a guy will be flattered that you think he is that important. He will feel like your hero and will be intoxicated by your attention. Then he will feel smothered, like he is buried under a pile of dirty socks. Eventually this will overwhelm him. Finally, he will find a way to get away from you. He may become angry, critical, or distant, or he may just stop caring and avoid you in any way he can. If you, as a girl, are driven by the need to be loved by a guy, chances are there is something unhealthy in your past that has made that need bigger than it is supposed to be. Pressuring a guy to love you deeply before he may be ready or capable is not going to make a hard thing easier.

On the flip side, guys with weak self-control pressure girls for all kinds of things. They can "steal" a girl's self-respect by dominating or controlling her. They might pressure girls to settle for a halfhearted effort toward the relationship on their part. But the most obvious example is sex. With roughly 86 percent of sexually active girls saying they wish they would have not had sex, it is usually the guy who puts undue pressure on a girl to do things that she isn't ready for and should not do.[3]

When it comes to dating, romance, and love, here is what you owe people: nothing. Love and dating should not be forced, and pressure doesn't exist in healthy relationships. If you are feeling obligated to do things that you aren't ready for by someone who says he cares about you, then you might want to consider what the word *care* means. Don't let people steal your lunch money. Or your Fruit Roll-Ups. Or your emotional health. They're yours, and they are worth a lot. Plus, Fruit Roll-Ups are really, really good.

Caution: Love Is Liquid Crack

I see addicts all the time. Usually they are addicted to things like "Jake" or "Haley." People in love bear a striking resemblance to drug addicts. And it turns out, so do their brains. When people are "in love," or at least are infatuated, their brains change dramatically. Three distinct areas of the brain become highly active. Brain scans highlight three areas: the *right ventral segmental area*, the *medial caudate nucleus*, and the *nucleus acumens*. I prefer to call them "the crazy tree," because they are lit up and connected like Christmas tree lights on a string. In addition, the chemicals they produce in your body cause a shortened attention span and affect your short-term memory as well as your goal-oriented behavior. You experience adrenaline rushes, your heart rate goes up, you can have trouble focusing, and you fixate on thoughts of another person in a way that really affects your geometry homework. The other time these areas of the brain activate like this is when someone is high on cocaine, crack, or other similarly addictive substances. This becomes especially noticeable when people become sexually involved. Their brains become addicted, driven, and even manic.[4] It doesn't stop there, however, as our brains can get into even more freaky behavior. Some parts of the brain stop functioning as productively as they used to. This can impair judgment and make people distrusting, anxious, and overanalyzing. When you add to this mix a drop in serotonin, which can increase obsessive-compulsive behavior, you can have one giant roller coaster of confusion.[5] All of these reactions find their best expression when there is real, sustained commitment. Commitment says, "It is safe to have these reactions, because I will always be there for you. Through the ups and downs of this roller coaster we call life, I will take the ride with you."

When people say that relationships are serious, and that you shouldn't be quick to jump into love and romance, they're not kidding. After all . . . love, passion, and infatuation are all very strong drugs; they just happen to be legal. So be careful with the "love drugs."

I wouldn't tell you these things without sharing my own personal dating experiences as well. I didn't really date heavily or seriously, and it turns out that was probably a good thing. When I look back at it, I'm glad I didn't. And I'm glad I didn't try to make the camp girl my girlfriend.

Camp Girl

There was a really pretty girl who was at my Young Life camp in high school. I was sixteen and pretty new to the social scene. I looked at the pretty girl and wondered if she would actually ever want to go on a date with me. I finally got the nerve up to ask her out when we got back home. I was so nervous I almost threw up, because let's face it, she probably had a lot of guys ask her out. I felt like a nervous chicken walking up to the wood block and putting my neck on the line. Would she say yes and make me a happy chicken, or say no and chop my head off, along with all my confidence? Luckily I held in the throw-up long enough to ask, and to my amazement, she said yes. I didn't care if it was pity, if she had a hard time saying no, or if she actually wanted to. I didn't care; she said yes.

I picked her up and thought that I was going to be amazed. I really hoped that she was the girl I imagined she was. Turns out, she wasn't. Not her fault; I just had a dreamy imagination. We couldn't talk about anything. She didn't care that I wanted to backpack all over the world someday. In fact, she didn't like camping at all, which I thought was ironic since we met at camp. She wanted to talk about being a fashion designer, and it was hard for me to get into that. We seriously didn't have anything in common other than that we both thought she was pretty. I was increasingly bummed to realize that even if we started dating, it would probably last one second. But as bummed as I was about it, it was a great thing to realize. We said good night that night, talked only one other time, and then went our separate ways. I learned about a personality type that was not a match for me romantically. And I'm sure she learned that same thing.

Moral of the story: don't force a relationship. If it's not going anywhere, then don't feel bad about walking away before it goes any further. There will always be another camp.

Magic Numbers of Dating

Some people say you shouldn't date at all, and some say you should date hundreds of people. Many people are somewhere in between. And all of the various opinions bring up an interesting question: is there a magic number of people you should date? Turns out some scientists think that there is . . . or at least there's a range . . .

It is between one and four. If you are part of the 95 percent of people who would like to get married, then certain social scientists believe this is the magic number of people you need to date before you marry.[6] Some pretty complex mathematical algorithms ~~formulas~~[7] figured this out, but I'll spare the boredom and tell you the point of them. If you are evaluating the qualities that you value and don't value in other people, you can pretty much find all of the important ones while dating somewhere between one and four people.

> MacKenzie: I like algorithms. Not real algorithms. Just the word.

> Chad: Yeah, I try to drop it casually in conversation . . . hoping that no one asks me to explain further . . .

This isn't really meant to give you tons of advice or to tell you how many people to date, but it is an interesting thought when you consider what the point of dating is: getting to know someone over an extended amount of time to determine if a romantic relationship is something worth pursuing. I thought if I said this twice, you might remember it more.

My Two-Week Wall

Let's say that Chad liked a girl. Let's call her Barb. She liked me too, and we hit it off pretty quickly. And that felt really exciting. Then we experienced all of those strange emotional things that happen when two people obviously like each other. We held hands, gazed at each other, and let's say, hypothetically, that we kissed a bit. And suddenly it happened. On the twenty-third hour of the sixth day of the second week, all my feelings suddenly ceased to exist. I no longer wanted to be Barb's boyfriend. There wasn't anything wrong with Barb; I just didn't want to be in the relationship anymore. Barb did not like this news. I felt like a jerk when I sat down with her and said that I

> MacKenzie: Did I change this word? I can't imagine you saying "bit" . . .
>
> Chad: Yeah, I did. It was between a "bit," a "smidgen," or a "teensy." I went with *not* the other two.
>
> MacKenzie: Maybe we should have checked the thesaurus . . .

didn't feel like we could date anymore. Then I used the line people always make fun of: "It's me, not you." But I actually meant it. This hurt her feelings, and I thought that I was really weird. I mean, how do feelings just disappear? Am I a jerk?

What I was actually doing, after having jumped into things too quickly, was protecting myself. I subconsciously realized very early on that I was not ready for a committed relationship. She thought she was. That meant that if I had stayed in the relationship, it would have gone deeper, and when it ended it would have hurt even more. Ideally, I would have figured this out sooner, before I affected her feelings at all. I sincerely never meant to hurt her, but I woke up and realized it was going nowhere. So I ended it. I decided not to fight for something that just couldn't work.

Barb is still a friend of mine, and I think we are both grateful now for not continuing the relationship. Sometimes you hit wall that has a big sign on it that says: "You are not ready." That wall is there to protect you.

BILL AND PAM

Cold Shoulder

Another of our sons was dating an amazing girl, when one day, after almost a year of dating, she started to ignore him. Being the nice, problem-solving guy he was, he kept asking her things like, "Did I do something wrong?" or "Is there something we need to talk about?" His friends said, "Dump her," but our son would never just walk away without talking things through.

When it came time for her birthday party, he spent a chunk of change to buy her a nice gift and do something really special for her. She completely ignored him and talked to every other guy there. Finally, to this girl's credit, she called and asked to talk, to explain how she was feeling. Yes, the breakup hurt, but not nearly as much as the hurt of watching her flirt with other guys and ignore him. If you want to date someone new, talk it out with the guy you are currently dating. It will save your heart and his if you are just honest with him.

It's Really Simple

Oh yeah, back to the main point . . . the thing you really need to know about dating. (I figured it out not from my own relationships, but from watching others'.)

I have a really close friend. (Thanks, I feel great about it too.) His name is Zach. We have been good friends for years, and I have had the pleasure of seeing him at his highs and his lows. This includes his experiences with girls. He was pretty crazy about a girl named Kelly. They really liked each other, and they started dating. Sweet, right? Well, not really. Even though they were nuts about each other, they argued a lot. He would get mad at her insecurities, and she would get frustrated because he wasn't living up to her expectations. So they broke up and went their separate ways. But they talked to each other from time to time and never really closed the door on their friendship, for whatever reason.

A couple of years went by, and they started talking more. The next thing you knew they were dating . . . again. But then I noticed something. He started getting frustrated again. So there they are, on dating try number two, and it still wasn't working. The reason I tell you this story is because I could tell that they sincerely liked each other. He was nuts about her, and he saw in Kelly the things he had always imagined in the girl he would marry. She had more feelings for Zach than she'd ever had for a guy . . .

Meanwhile, Chad was getting annoyed. I wanted to punch myself in the face having to listen to all of this. It was a neverending cycle. Zach was mad at Kelly. She was mad at him. He thought she flirted with too many guys. She didn't like his friends. He hated her dog. I could go on, but I will spare you the one thousand details that got me thinking of inflicting pain on myself as an alternative to hearing about their miserable relationship. They kept trying, but they weren't getting anywhere. They were exhausting each other. And me.

So one day Zach asked me if he should just end it, even though he didn't want to. I thought about it, then simply said, "Yes . . . absolutely." He looked surprised. Really surprised. But when you come down to it, it's only a yes or a no. He was either going to end up marrying her one day, or he was not. He asked me why I gave such a simple and absolute answer. And I told him why with six words:

"Relationships are supposed to be good."

If God designed our relationships and they are supposed to reflect him, benefit us, and help us love one another and understand God more, then they should be good. They should not be negative and frustrating *the majority of the time*. I said to Zach, "Hey, man, you know dating is supposed to be fun, right? Relationships can be like a broken glass; sometimes it can be better to leave it broken than to hurt yourself trying to put it back together." And just because he and Kelly had both invested time, energy, and emotion didn't mean that they were supposed to be together.

The truth is this: dating is actually pretty easy. Ask any married couple if it gets more complicated or less complicated when you move from dating to marriage. I promise you they will laugh and then answer you quickly. People shouldn't walk away from marriage, but dating is not marriage. Dating is supposed to be the time when you get to know someone and just enjoy that person. And if you really match up with each other, you should be able to step back and say, "This is a positive experience. It makes me more kind, loving, diverse, happy, closer to God, balanced, and generally a healthier person who is growing in life." If this is not your experience, perhaps you shouldn't be in that relationship.

There is someone great out there for Zach to enjoy. There's someone for Kelly too. But neither Zach's nor Kelly's "someone" will be each other.

Relationships are not designed so that you have to manage heartbreak. That is not what God wants for you. He wants you to thrive in them, not just deal with them. And when you think about dating, keep this simple thought in mind: dating should be positive. It won't always be easy, but the overall tone of the relationship should be a positive one. If it's not, then rethink how you are doing it or who you are doing it with.

CHAPTER 9

Study Before the Test

Do not be misled: "Bad company corrupts good character."

—1 CORINTHIANS 15:33

If you want to have a positive dating experience, don't think it just happens. Remember my wood-shop bridge? If you try to just wing it, odds are that it won't go as well as it could. You have to plan ahead of time and understand the road you are getting ready to travel on.

Are You Ready to Date?

Before you take your driver's test, you study for the exam. In the same way, you should probably think through some things about dating before you get in the driver's seat of relationships. You don't want to wreck the car. So consider these stop signs ahead in case you have taken the wheel or are about to.

The Rebel Dater

If you start dating because you are mad at your parents and want to show your independence and gain some freedom, then odds are you are a rebellious dater. While it's natural to want more independence as you get older, this is not a good reason to be dating. It's not fair to the person you're dating, and most likely your behavior will be more conflict driven and extreme, and you'll find someone who is more opposed to the views of your parents than in agreement with them.

Dating for a Daddy

I'm sorry, I know that sounds really gross and creepy, but there are a phenomenal number of girls looking for love to replace the love that they are not getting from their fathers. Not having a father's love creates a big void in people, and tragically, a girl will often try to replace the love she has not gotten from her father with a boyfriend. This will fail. The person you are dating cannot fill the void and love that you need from a father. I personally believe that our heavenly Father fills the void that our earthly fathers may fall short of, and he begs us to come to him before we make the mistake of looking for that love and affirmation in a boyfriend or anything else. A boyfriend is not your father.

The Serial Dater

For those who can't spell, this has nothing to do with break-fast *cereal*. This is the person who constantly jumps from relationship to relationship and develops a habit of *having* to be in a relationship. This is bad.

The younger you start dating and the more often you date

people, the higher your odds are of experiencing unhealthy relationship habits, negative feelings, depression, a poor self-image, sexual abuse, rape, less relationship satisfaction, and a long list of other bad stuff, including a higher risk of suicide. I cringe when a thirteen-year-old comes up to me and says, "Okay, so I've had a long string of bad relationships," because it is immediately obvious to me that he or she is at high risk of experiencing very negative relationships, heartache, and unhappiness.

Quality is way better than quantity, especially where relationships are concerned.

Sexual Abuse

The stats are overwhelming, and it's important to stop and think about them. One in four girls and one in six guys have been in some way sexually abused.[1] If this has happened to you, I am sorry. It's not your fault, and it's terrible. But you need to know it will affect your relationships. You cannot have healthy relationships until you talk about your abuse and try to deal with it. This affects the very core of people whether they want to believe it or not. Please strongly consider talking to someone and learning more about overcoming it. Do not be ashamed, and know that God loves you and can heal you from these things if you take the first step and bring the issue to the light. I say this so that you can eventually enjoy the wonderful relationships that God has in store for you.

> If you've been abused, please visit www.loveisrespect.org/. Don't wait another day to get help.

Missionary Daters

This term describes people who date others with very different religious and social viewpoints from their own with the hope of "converting" them. But here is the problem: it doesn't usually work, and it's also not the point of dating.

Dating doesn't exist so that you can change someone or force him or her to see your point of view. It's kind of like standing on a chair and trying to help someone up onto that chair. It's easier for the person to pull you off the chair than it is to help the person onto it.

> MacKenzie: I don't really think there are any benefits you can get from dating as a teen that you really can't get from a great friendship. Just my opinion.

> Chad: Well, you won't relate to all the teen romantic comedies as well . . . but I also think that's true. Just my opinion.

A lot of times Christians wonder whether or not it's a good idea to date someone who doesn't believe the same things as them. And the simple answer is: no. You are better off being that person's friend than his or her significant other, because you can be a friend to all people, and it won't compromise your moral or faith basis.

Older Guys + Younger Girls = Bad News

The average age difference for married couples in the United States is just over two years. The average difference in age between teen girls who get pregnant and the guys who get them pregnant is 6.2 years.[2] This is awful and extremely unfortunate. That means in most cases it is considered statutory rape as well. That also means that they don't have much in common and are experiencing very different parts of life. Many girls report that guys older than them are more mature than guys their age, and this seems more appealing. The greater the age difference, especially as teenagers, the more dominating and controlling the guy's behavior is in the relationship, and the higher correlation there is to all the bad stuff I mentioned earlier, like pregnancy, depression and so on. I have seen thirty-year-olds seduce and manipulate seventeen-year-olds; these things happen often. You have to become smart and not be naïve about age differences—they usually represent differences in life experience. And the closer in life experience you are with someone, the healthier and more balanced the relationship will be. "He really likes me, though," is a statement I hear daily. It doesn't matter. It's bad news.

> Above all else, guard your heart, for it is the wellspring of life.
>
> —Proverbs 4:23

Where Should We Go?

Okay, so you've found a nice, healthy person (who does not fit in any of the above categories) to date . . . now where should you go? What should you do? Active dates in public places or with lots of people are safer and healthier than the "let's just go somewhere dark and be alone and put in a movie that we won't really watch" dates. Those dates are almost as bad as a "let's just lie on your bed and talk about our feelings and look at your pictures" date. Guys only have one association with girls and lying on a bed, and it doesn't involve praying or looking at pictures.

Here are ten great (and active) date ideas:

1. Some sports make great date options. Even if you have no athletic ability, you can at least get some exercise and laugh together. A few to try: ice-skating, tennis, bowling, biking, or simply walking.

2. Do what the tourists do. What is your area known for? Go to the zoo, museum, or other historical or noteworthy site. (Especially if there is something that interests your date.)

> MacKenzie: I find it interesting that Chad and the Farrels all suggested feeding ducks! I've never fed ducks on a date before . . . hmmm . . .
>
> Chad: What are you going to say next, you've never gone to Disneyland? Come on! Feeding ducks rocks my face in two.
>
> MacKenzie: I haven't been to Disneyland, actually. Just Disney World.

3. Go to the park. Swing and talk, fly a kite, or take some bread to feed the ducks. Pack a picnic.

4. Go to a seasonal farm and pick apples, berries, or pumpkins.

5. Go shopping or browsing at the mall or interesting shopping districts.

What are five dates you think would be a lot of fun?

1.

2.

3.

4.

5.

Where Shouldn't We Go?

Even more important than having a plan for what you will do on your dates is knowing the places you won't go. I've already given you two really bad date ideas; what are some other people, places, and activities that you think should *always* be avoided?

Things I will *never* do on a date:

_____

_____

P.S. if you actually take time to think about these things and write them down, then you will be infinitely better off than if you don't. Writing something down makes it more likely to happen—or not happen. And that's important concerning your boundaries.

Good or Bad

Remember that dating can be good or bad, fantastic or horrible, and the experience will be up to you. Because these things don't happen incidentally or just randomly, all of our relationships, dates, and boyfriends or girlfriends are a culmination of our decisions. And much like a sound building or a sturdy bridge, it takes time, planning, effort, and development to build them so that they will become what they were meant to be. Make your choices carefully and wisely, because you make your choices, and your choices end up making you.

BILL AND PAM

Remember, Guys Have Feelings Too

Ditched at the Dance: Some people might think that a painful hit or the loss of a big game would be the most obvious way to hurt a big football star. Surprisingly, it's way easier to do it through their emotions. Our son—polite, respectful of girls, and a gentleman—was dumped, ditched, and abandoned at his senior homecoming dance when his girlfriend left with another guy. Not only did she take off with another guy, she took our son's car keys and some of his friends' car keys that were in her purse. He had to call us to come pick him up, along with all the kids who were coming to the after party at our house. Then he had to call the girl's parents and tell them that their daughter had left with some other guy, and he wasn't sure exactly who he was or where they were going. Our son volunteered to go look for her. He found her, took her home, and broke up with her on the way. The guy who never cried came home and sobbed into his mom's arms.

His *ex*-girlfriend didn't give him any reasons why she treated him so badly. It might have hurt if she had said earlier, "I want to go to the dance with someone else." But it would have hurt a whole lot less than the public humiliation he went through that night, and the fear he felt when he had to go search for a girl he felt responsible for, having promised her parents he'd return her home safely. If you want to transition in your relationships, talk about it, but don't hurt people. Girls have sensitive feelings, and guys really do have feelings too.

May I Suggest Something?

Well, I'm going to anyway. When it comes to high school and junior high, I strongly recommend the following: worry about having friends, not boyfriends or girlfriends. You might laugh this off, but I still say it confidently, and here is why: I almost *never* get a letter or have someone tell me of all the wonderful benefits of the teenage relationships that he or she is in. If I get any one positive letter about teen boyfriends or girlfriends, it's only after I get five *hundred* about all the negative stuff. I wish it weren't this way, but it is. Sure, dating can help you understand the things you like and don't like about people, but it seems as though it's hard to keep it that simple. People often find themselves falling too deeply into emotional situations, and they would have been better off just waiting until they were older. I can't really tell you many positive things that come from young dating relationships, but I can tell you another book's worth of information about all of the problems that seem to result from it. I don't hear people saying, "You know, I just wish I had spent a lot more time in relationships in high school and having a lot more boyfriends/girlfriends." But I constantly hear, "I wish I would have spent more time with friends and learning about myself instead of on high school dating relationships."

High school dating relationships don't usually last, but high school friends can. And friendship is something that is probably more beneficial and enjoyable than the other stuff anyway. When you learn how to be a friend, you are actually making yourself healthier, happier, and way more appealing and attractive to people. Maybe you'll believe me, maybe you won't, but I hope you'll at least consider it. Because when it comes to your life and your relationships, I look forward to the day that I start getting more letters that say, "I'm really happy."

CHAPTER 10

Shoot Your Barber

You cannot shake hands with a clenched fist.

—INDIRA GANDHI

Conflict (v). 1. to come into a disagreement; be contradictory, at variance, or in opposition; clash or dissent. 2. (n). dispute of action, feeling, or effect; antagonism or opposition, as of interests or principles; for example, a conflict of ideas. 3. (n). when your brain and their brain want to fight!

When I was a freshman, I was awkward. Now you know. I had been in a long-term therapy and rehab program because of a bunch of bad circumstances and bad decisions. I stayed there for a long time, and when they thought I was ready, I was sent back to high school, where I was awkward in all kinds of new ways. I didn't really know how to be social like the other kids. They knew how to interact with each other, they knew the teachers, they knew who the quiet kids were, and they knew who the loud, obnoxious kids were. I did not.

I decided I would work really hard and get good grades. I really wanted to change. I thought a good way to start was to get an A instead of an F in biology. But there were a couple of problems in my class . . . .

Both of these problems had funny hair. They went by Sean and R. J. They sat in front of me and interrupted the teacher and made fun of people. They were really good at it, and no one really said anything to them. Enter clueless Chad. They were so distracting that I couldn't concentrate; they never shut up. So one day I said, "Hey, will you be quiet, please?" There. Problem solved, right? No. Bad social decision, as I'm sure you understand instantly. So I did the only thing that I knew to do at the time; I struck back. I looked at Sean's longer bowl-cut, skater hair and said, "Shoot your barber, man." Of course he laughed and said, "Okay, shoot my barber. Really, that's all you can say? Good one." The next day when he said something mean to me, I said, "Shoot your barber." This went on for months. It wasn't really that effective, but there was a conflict, and I had no idea how to deal with it. As it turned out, it wasn't just awkward Chad who didn't know how to deal with conflict. Whether it was an annoying kid in biology, an argument with a girlfriend, or frustrating parents, almost no one in class really knew how to deal with the problems they had with others. But, as it turns out, there are actually some things you can learn to help you deal with conflict.

Somehow, Sean and I became friends. More than ten years later, he is still one of my best friends, and he was even in my wedding. Every now and then we still say, "Hey, man, shoot your barber." ◄ - - - - - - - - - - - - - -

If you go through life without conflict, there is probably something wrong with you. Gandhi, my grandma, and Jesus experienced conflict. My goldfish fight, my cousin told me I was ugly and dumb, two dogs in my front yard were fighting

> Mackenzie: That's pretty funny. I think you have come a long way with your sarcasm techniques since then.

> Chad: That's one of the best compliments I have ever heard. Ever. Thank you.

the other day, and I promise, you will have conflict too. But conflict does not have to destroy relationships. Conflict can, in fact, heighten your understanding of what is really important in relationships.

Why We Fight

As a teenager, you are at a very unique time in your life. Your entire brain and body are transforming in new ways, and this in turn causes certain stresses in your life. In addition, it becomes more difficult at times to manage your reactions to people and life because you haven't felt or dealt with certain things before. Social pressures, boyfriend and girlfriend issues, your parents' expectations, wondering if you are smart, wondering if you are athletic, wondering if you are funny, wondering if you are good-looking, and dealing with your surging hormones can sometimes push you over the edge . . .

To resolve conflict in your life, you have to want to do it, you have to know how to do it, and sometimes you just have to out-last the obstacles like Sean and I did. Learning to deal with conflict will take the most effort on your part, so let's take a look at what works when it comes to handling conflict. Here are some simple things to consider:

Walk Away

Seriously, walk away for a while if things get heated. This can be very hard to do, but it's important. Conflicts can't be solved in the face of boiling emotions. When I am mad, I have to take at least a few minutes by myself. Don't use the time to sit and brew and plan an attack, even a verbal one. It won't resolve your issue. Instead, give yourself some time to calm down and figure out what happened and to find ways to cre-ate a winning compromise. Plus, walking is good exercise. So walk away.

Don't Be an Honest Jerk

A lot of teenagers run their mouths without realizing it. "What? I'm just being honest" is a common explanation for this statement. This might be true, but you can be honest and still be a jerk, a mean person, or just rude. Sometimes those words run right into other people's feelings and upset them. Honesty without compassion can easily be taken as harsh criti-cism. So before words come out of your mouth, even if you think you are just being honest, make sure that you are being sensitive too. Would you want someone to say to you what you're about to say? And don't say you don't care; you do. A little sensitivity will help reduce the misunderstandings and conflicts in your life.

Shut Your Mouth and Open Your Ears

People who are great at conflict resolution have mastered a simple concept: talk less and listen more. People who are quick to say what they think will experience more difficult times. When people are quick to listen, it shows that they care, which is perhaps the easiest way to set a course toward resolution. Listening is powerful; it gives more clarity than simply talking. So perk up those ears when you are in a rough spot. It might serve you well.

Rearrange Your Alphabet

Replace the letter *U* with *I*. The best way to throw gasoline on the fire of an argument is to say "you this, and you that."

"I messages" are tools for expressing how we feel without attacking or blaming. By starting with "I," we take responsibility for the way we perceive the problem. This is the exact opposite of "you messages," which put others on the defensive and close doors to communication. Statements like, "You never listen to me. You never consider how anyone else is feeling!" only escalate things.

When making "I" statements, it's important to avoid put-downs, guilt trips, sarcasm, or negative body language. Keep in mind, "It's us against the problem, not us against each other." So try saying, "I'm frustrated because I don't feel listened to." While this sounds like a tiny difference, I promise you that it will save you hours of arguing. While there is no *I* in *team*, there is an *I* in *fight*. And the more you use "I" statements while dealing with conflict, the happier *you* will be.

Say You're Sorry

I cut someone off while driving my car on the highway. I didn't mean to; I just wasn't paying attention, and he wasn't clearly in my side-view mirror. It was my bad. He didn't like what I did at all and decided to let me know. He quickly pulled into the other lane, sped up, and drove aggressively close to my car. Our windows were down, and he was yelling at me—and I'm pretty sure he wasn't saying he thought my eyes were pretty. Then he waved his middle finger at me and told me I was number one. I just kind of looked at him and said, "I'm really sorry." His face instantly changed. He went from rage to silence. Then he looked back at me and just said, "Oh, okay," and waved at me and backed off.

If you do something wrong . . . apologize. The words "I'm sorry" convey responsibility and will more quickly move the situation toward forgiveness for all involved.

Oh yeah, if you want to ever be happy when you get married one day, roughly two million percent of married couples say that these are important words to learn.

You Pushed My Giant Button

What really irritates you? Sometimes simply knowing some of the buttons that cause conflict in your life will help you tremendously. Here are a couple of mine:

- Using "always" and "never." "You *always* do that Chad!" You can't always or never do anything, and every time I hear these words, I want to scream at the person who said them rather than work anything out.
- Cutting me off midsentence or talking loudly over me. I am not even sure why this one bugs me, but I can tell you that I gain an instant desire to duct tape someone's mouth shut.

- Being late for no reason, constantly. I sit there waiting for someone, feeling like a dork.
- Being mean to or making fun of someone physically, or because of the way a person looks. That's my rage button.

What are some of your buttons? Are they realistic frustrations, or are they things you will need to change about yourself first?

Your Perspective—Only One of Many

Most of the time people don't tell me I'm a jerk, but I'll tell myself that on occasion. And it's usually for good reason. Sometimes, I only see my side of the story . . .

In college, this girl and I were partners on a project. Several days before its due date, she stopped e-mailing me, wouldn't pick up her phone, and didn't send me her portion of the project. Over the next two days, I began to get really mad, and I started thinking about how selfish and thoughtless she was. She had forgotten a few things before, so I called and left her a really frustrated message saying that I couldn't believe she was blowing off our project, because it was going to affect my grade. Then I got an e-mail from her that said, "Hey, I'm sorry about the class stuff. I'll try to get it to you later. My dad died in a wreck this weekend, and I had to fly home. I'll get you that work as soon as I can." Chad = Instant Giant Jerk. That is exactly how I felt. I had only considered the possibilities from my point of view.

We don't know everything. We don't know what other people are going through, but if we stop to think before we react and remember that issues may exist below the surface, we can show a lot more empathy. It's way better to know the story and get perspective than to be an insensitive jerk. Trust me.

Conflict Is Good

Conflict is not bad, if you and the opposing party are willing to take responsibility for your actions, what you did wrong, and try to learn from it. If you are able to learn, listen, apologize, and convey your thoughts and feelings, you will find that while conflict is not fun, it can bring people closer. If you see every conflict as a way to learn about yourself and other people, then you will have less of it. And when you do have it . . . you can learn to express your care for other people. And people like that.

B.E. Aggressive . . . or Don't Be

As far as I can see, there are three distinctive styles of dealing with conflict. One of these styles is really good and will set you up to have great relationships. The other two, although common, don't work very well if your goal is to actually have friends. Knowing which style you use will help you figure out where you need to grow in this area. Knowing which type others use will help you know how to best deal with a difficult situation. So here are a few.

The Passive Approach

Passive people have trouble communicating and standing up for their needs. They may be afraid to stand up for themselves, either because their self-worth is low, they lack good communication skills, or they simply don't like conflict. As a result, these people may be more likely to be bullied or taken advantage of. Their approach is often to avoid the conflict or to give in so they don't have to deal with it. If you are this type of person, you wish I had never even brought up this subject.

The Aggressive Approach

Aggressive people are often confrontational and intimidating in their personal interactions. They use threatening words or body language and can be very unaware of the other person's needs. Their sole goal is to get what they want. Cooperation is difficult for them, and their interactions with people may be abrasive. They may resort to name-calling or threats more easily. Their approach is to do whatever they need to do to get their way, often at the expense of other people's feelings. If you have this approach, you probably think you have a better way of explaining this than I do.

The Assertive Approach

Assertive people know how to get their needs met while respecting the needs of others. They display balance. They know how to cooperate and compromise, and their goal is to achieve a win-win outcome. Their approach is to listen to others but still make their own needs and ideas known. This is the ideal approach to use in most situations.[1]

One More Thing

Forgiveness Is Awesome . . . and Dumb

Forgiveness is one of the greatest skills you can develop in your life. I can guarantee that people will say and do things that will hurt you, disappoint you, and leave you feeling like yesterday's leftovers. If, however, you get really good at forgiving, you will feel positive about yourself despite how others act, and you will stay on track with what you are best at and not get stuck dwelling on past pain you have experienced. Most important, forgiveness keeps you from allowing other people's mistakes to ruin the course of your life.

Luckily forgiveness is a decision and doesn't require the people who have hurt you to do anything before you can start feeling better. In fact, it is usually less about the other person and more about you anyway. It's the practice of forgiving that will help you let go, not hold grudges, and grow as a person and in relationships. And just for future reference, forgiveness gives us the ability to stay in love for a lifetime. Nobody is perfect, and all great relationships are made up of two committed forgivers.

But don't be dumb about certain relationships. And don't be naïve. Forgiving is good, but that doesn't mean you can fix every relationship. Sometimes you need to forgive and walk away. Here's how it works: if someone wrongs you, you need to forgive him or her. If that person also says he or she is sorry, you can try to give the relationship another chance. But if that person only says the words and doesn't back it up with action, then you should protect yourself and walk away. Too many people allow themselves to be taken advantage of because they want to forgive. Just make sure you balance your smarts with your hearts.

Pam's Word on PMS and the Pasta Princess

Chad and Bill bailed on this topic, but thought I might have a few words of wisdom since I'm a girl. I know PMS is real; trust me girls, but I also know that it doesn't have to control us or add unnecessary conflict to our lives.

Here are a few ways to know you might have PMS:

1. Everyone around you has an attitude problem.

2. You're adding chocolate chips to your cheese omelet.

3. The dryer has shrunk every last pair of your jeans.

Pray for Power
Make a Plan
Seek Some Fun

Pray: You will feel edgy, bloated, irritable, emotional, anxious, and maybe even angry. Just because you feel like you have the flu and you've been hit by a bus doesn't mean you need to take it out on everyone else. Ask God to help you choose to be nice, even if you don't feel nice. Even if you are not feeling 100 percent, do the right thing anyway. Besides, we can't let a little biology slow us down, right girls? In one of the Olympics, an American swimmer won three gold medals and broke a world record while at the height of her period. [2]

Make a Plan: Decide ahead of time to handle your symptoms proactively. Things that help include sleep, a bubble bath (or soak in a Jacuzzi), avoiding sugary and salty foods (the exact things you are craving!), and staying away from soft drinks and caffeine. You are already amped up emotionally, so that enormous cup of mocha may just send you further over the edge!

Instead of fast food, eat salads, veggies, fresh fruit, whole grains, and lean protein. Drink lots of water too. And take your vitamins, because calcium supplements and B complex vitamins will help you feel better. [3]

Another thing that might help is to record how you feel for four months. Every day, write down how you feel emotionally and physically. I just write a number on my calendar, one to ten, with ten meaning I am in total near-death misery and one meaning I feel fantastic. If you do this for several months, you will know which days on your cycle are your hardest and you can give yourself a little slack those days.

Seek Some Fun: Get active. In *Why Men and Women Act the Way They Do*, I quote some doctors' advice:

Doctors don't know for sure why exercise helps PMS, but some believe that it helps stabilize blood sugar. Getting active may also increase endorphins, the body's relaxing hormones that are five-hundred times more potent than morphine. A brisk twenty or thirty minute walk three times a week seems to be enough to help most women.

Exercise reduces stress, raises serotonin levels, and increases oxygen in the blood and the blood flow, which helps reduce water retention. By strengthening muscles, it can prevent lower back pain and cramps. Try walking, swimming, bicycling, tennis, or moderate jogging three times a week; increase activity the week before your symptoms usually begin.[4]

Try to enjoy things you know you love on PMS days: spending time with friends, listening to uplifting songs, or watching a funny movie.

If these things don't help, talk to your mom or a responsible female adult in your life about the problem.

PMS, Her Period, and You—A Bit of Advice for the Guys

Guys raised with sisters have a little edge when it comes to having some insight into the female cycle. If you don't have sisters, here are some clues that a woman might be having PMS:

- She considers chocolate a major food group.
- She says, "What mood?!" as she pulls out a semi-automatic rifle.
- You ask her to please pass the salt at the table and she blurts, "DO I HAVE TO DO EVERYTHING?"
- She orders three burgers, four large fries, a bucket of fried chicken, and a milk shake from Dairy Queen and then chews out the convenient store guy because they're out of diet soda.

Seriously, what's a guy to do?

- **Get a clue**: Learn what happens to a woman during her menstrual cycle. Every twenty-eight days you'll need to deal with it once you are in a serious relationship, so get informed now. As her body releases an egg and it floats down her tubes to exit her body, her hormones fire off all kinds of directives. She retains water just in case one of those eggs gets fertilized and she becomes a mother. Her body becomes tense, and she might feel as horrible as you do after two-a-days during football season—only she has to feel that way every month for most of her life. If you felt that bad that often, you might be a little grumpy too. She might also experience cramps before and during her period. Emotionally, the week before her period she can feel sad, angry, anxious, scared, overwhelmed, tired, or a host of other emotions all mixed together.

- **Offer some compassion**: A little sympathy goes a long way with a girl. If you are nice to her on her less-than-perfect days, she will remember it with fondness.

- **Get a thick skin**: Your sister, mother, or girlfriend might say or do things that seem kind of, well, mean. It is okay to offer a gentle reminder to her that she hurt your feelings, but try not to take things she says during this time personally. She will be back to expressing her feelings and opinions in a kinder, more compassionate way in a few days.

People Matter

Are you a human who has feelings? Yes, you are. I'm guessing you already know that. However, people seem to forget this about each other all the time. No matter what is happening to you in your life, things are happening in others' lives too. And a lot of stuff in people's lives can be tough. Everyone encounters frustrating situations with people, but not everyone stops for a second to remember one simple thing: all people are valuable. God does not care any less about them than he does about you. They have feelings, hearts, and sensitive issues in their lives. And they all deserve to be treated with these things in mind. Sometimes, if I can remember that, I look at an argument with a different set of eyes: the set that sees with compassion. Conflict will always exist. How we experience it is determined by us. Remember, conflict involves two people, and both people should be considered.

CHAPTER 11

Dolphin Sex Ed

To let a fool kiss you is stupid. To let a kiss fool you is worse.

—E. Y. HARBURG

I once read that dolphins and humans were two of the only species that had sex just for the sake of pleasure. This meaning that we, the humans, will have sexual intercourse at times when it is impossible for the female to get pregnant. And this got me thinking about what pleasure and sex actually exist for. It also made me feel kind of funny about dolphins . . . but that's probably my own issue.

There are very few species that have sex outside of their

> Mackenzie: You would think I would no longer be surprised at your randomness. And yet . . . how you integrated dolphins and humans into an exclusive sex club is beyond me.

> Chad: It's a pretty complicated method of a lack of sleep, Cheez-Its, and watching a lot of National Geographic. But I'll just take that as a compliment.

reproductive cycles, just for the bonding and physical pleasure that it encapsulates. Two of these are dolphins and humans. Our brain structure is highly developed and similar in nature. It's kind of an exclusive club we're a part of, in a weird way, if you think about it. Which you probably don't.

Dolphins and their sexual habits really aren't the main point . . . you are. Which brings up the topic of sex and leads me to a very important point concerning waffles and spaghetti.

Waffle Sex Is *Not* Spaghetti Sex

This is probably the most important thing to remember in this chapter, so I'll just say it right up front. Guys and girls have a ton of similarities and a ton of differences. You might have picked up on this by now . . . it's kind of the point of the book. And there is no better example than this:

Guys and girls have sex for different reasons!

There is a fundamental difference. And it has to do with the word *love*. This is not always the case, but a general rule is this: *Guys give love in order to get sex. Girls give sex in order to get love.* If you are married, it's no big deal; this actually works out to be a pretty fair balance. When you are married, you are a lot less likely to break up. Marriage is potentially the most stable relationship that can exist, and it completely changes how sex is experienced. Outside of marriage, sex gets complicated.

Whenever I ask a roomful of guys why people have sex, there are always several guys who immediately and loudly yell, "Cause it feels good!" For guys, physical satisfaction is the defining motivation for sex. While sex can be an emotional experience for guys, it pales in comparison to how emotional sex is for girls.

Imagine the waffle again. Guys compartmentalize sex in one of these boxes. Guys don't yell, "Because you are in love" as a reason to have sex. The one time a guy said this, another guy yelled, "Nice answer, loser." Guys, especially as teenagers, do not equate love and sex.

For girls, sex and deep connection are one and the same. The female body releases oxytocin, a chemical hormone that bonds a girl to her partner during sex. If a girl becomes an emotional wreck after she sleeps with her boyfriend and is later dumped, she doesn't respond this way by choice. She developed an emotional, physical, and chemical bond to that person. Girls cannot compartmentalize sex as just another thing. Girls who try to do this are usually coping with bad relationships, sexual abuse, or some other trauma that happened to them earlier in life. While teenage guys are not usually equating sex and love, girls are. After all, sex is the physical act of love; it is not just a physical gratification. A girl cannot compartmentalize these deep and complicated things, nor should she. Guys don't equate sex to love. Girls usually do. Outside of marriage, this will inevitably create heartache.

The Collision of Perspectives

Take one person who is not thinking long-term and one person who is; then add sex. The result, as you can probably guess, is a train wreck.

Guys are more intrigued by girls that they have to pursue. Guys like the chase. Really, they do. And luckily, girls like to be pursued. And the harder a guy works for something—a car, a good grade, or a girl—the more he values it. If you give a boy something, he might appreciate it. But if he has to work for it, he will cherish it.

Sex is the most intimate way a girl can be discovered. When a guy gets to this point easily, or without having to sacrifice much more than a handful of dates, a couple of months, and a few conversations, he will become bored. It wasn't hard to get, so it must not be that valuable. This fact might upset people and sometimes confuse girls, but it doesn't make it any less true.

> A teenage relationship will end in less than four weeks, on average, after you bring sex into it.

Guys are not thinking about deep, long-term commitment or marriage in high school. They are not! This leads to incredibly deep frustration for girls. But the truth is, it's better that the guys are not thinking about deep commitment. They are not ready for it.

You shouldn't make a child try to run before he can hardly walk. He will fall and hurt himself. And you shouldn't introduce physically powerful things like sex into a relationship until you are in a place that nurtures the things that it awakens in people, which, by the way, works best in marriage.

The Physical Side of Sex

The male waffle brain has about twice the capacity for sex-related thinking. Guys do, in fact, have sex on their minds more often than girls. The area in the hypothalamus for sexual pursuit is larger in guys because testosterone causes it to grow larger. When puberty hits, between the ages of nine and fifteen, the guy receives another huge batch of testosterone. This, in turn, increases his awareness of touch, taste, smell, and other cognitive systems and strengthens their connection with sex.[1]

And the result is a guy who is very, very, very aware of the female body. Guys might get involuntary erections while simply sitting in class, and there is nothing they can do to make them go away. Almost all guys at some point will joke about having to walk down the halls with their books in front of their bodies. It's okay, fellas . . . every guy has been there.

Girls have the same connections in their brains devoted to sex as guys, but they're about half the size. Females, biologically, do not devote as much mental time and effort to sexual pursuit.

The Bible Route

For some people, religion shapes their view on sex. Many people go to church and simply hear that sex outside of marriage is a sin. But it's not always explained *why* it is a sin. Even if you don't attend church, then you still might hear a variety of messages against premarital sex. The strongest message against it is that you can get pregnant or contract one of the twenty-five varieties of STDs and STIs.[2] The most common message about the appropriate time for sex is simply to wait until you are "ready." Since you are technically physically able or "ready" to have sex around age eleven or twelve, this doesn't really make any sense. Not to mention the fact that sex causes babies, and fourteen-year-olds are not ready to be parents. Feelings change constantly, so "feeling ready" is actually a terrible way to gauge when someone should have sex. This vague standard does not help people, and it only ends up confusing things even more. It makes more sense to ask, "Am I treating my sexuality as valuable as it actually is?"

If you are a youth group pro, you might have heard it said that God wants people to wait for sex until marriage. But you still may not know why. Whether or not you go to youth group, the principles in the Bible *do*, in fact, make a lot of sense. In the fourth chapter of 1 Thessalonians, the Bible talks about avoiding sexual immorality. Notice it does not say sexual intercourse. It's not talking about a rule. It is talking about a principle. It also says we should learn self-control and that we are to treat ourselves and others in a holy and honorable way. The Bible was written in Hebrew and Greek, and when you go back to the original meaning, it's fascinating. *Honor* in Greek is *timh*, and when people used that word, they meant things like, "dignity, high price, valuable, precious, of value, and high esteem." This word is meant to convey that you, your body, and your emotions are highly valuable. You are worth something, and a great lot of something at that. So treat yourself and others with dignity and with high value.

So even if you have heard "because God says so," you can always look at the reasons *why* God says so. They make a lot of sense, they go beyond some simple religious rule to keep you from having fun, and they always have you in mind. God is pretty thoughtful that way.

Street Cred

This is important. Well, maybe not your street credit, but your reputation. You cannot keep your actions from the observations of others. Therefore you cannot separate your behavior and your reputation. And unfortunately, having sex does not usually make your reputation better. Yes, I know that there is a double standard here. Guys don't get called sluts and whores. If they do, it doesn't really bother them. This is not true of girls. In the reputation department, girls suffer more. But it still matters for both genders. If a guy has a bad reputation, and his dream girl comes along and realizes that he is sleazy or a player, it hurts her opinion of him. If a guy meets a girl that he is crazy about but finds out that people tease her about being a slut, or people say she is easy, his opinion of her will change.

It's easier to build a good reputation than it is to try to *re*build it.

Here is an example of a letter that I have *not* received.

> Hey Chad,
>
> I just want you to know that I have slept with a couple of guys in my school. One was my boyfriend of six months and the other was just a casual thing. I really loved it and things have been great since. I feel like I get more respect from girls and guys, and I have just fallen in love with myself since then. I have learned about how important my body is, and after these experiences, I just feel more valuable. Sex has been sooo great, I can't wait to keep having it.

But here *is* a letter that I have received, along with about fifteen-hundred others like it.

Here's the problem, Chad,

I'm SICK OF GUYS. I'm sick of them for a couple
of reasons. The main one is because I made a mistake
and I slept with two different guys. But I didn't think
it would ruin my life. Now guys at my school won't leave
me alone. They harass me at my locker at school, I
have things shot down my shirt all the time, I have
my butt grabbed about twenty times a day, and I know
that I'm an easy target. It's like I did one thing and my
whole life changed.

I tell them to stop all the time, but I just can't get
them to, and I've told billions of teachers who don't do
anything. All the girls think I'm a slut because of it, and
I hate it. I have like two girlfriends and fifteen guy
ones. I just don't know what to do anymore.

Please help!
Laney

Like it or not, your actions will help determine your reputation. Be careful with them.

It's *Not* About *Not* Doing Something

It's not my job to tell you what to do or what not to do, and so I
won't spend my time telling you not to do things. That decision
is up to you. Check out this chart, which shows the possible
physical expressions you can experience in your sex life throughout your life.

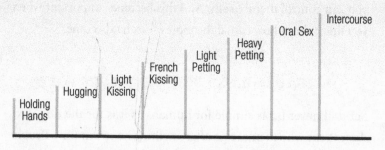

Holding Hands | Hugging | Light Kissing | French Kissing | Light Petting | Heavy Petting | Oral Sex | Intercourse

Increased Intimacy and Vulnerability ➝

Each of these options is good when expressed at the right time in your life. The challenge is trying to figure out when the right time is. Take a minute to draw your own lines on the chart. Where would you draw it in a friendship, casual dating relationship, and a girlfriend/boyfriend relationship? What will you save for marriage? As you think through your decisions, consider these words, "Above all else, guard your heart, for it is the wellspring of life" (Proverbs 4:23). The sexual part of who you are is valuable, and it is tied to your heart. When you guard your sex life, you guard your heart.

> God's will is for you to be holy, so stay away from all sexual sin.
>
> —1 Thessalonians 4:3 (NLT)

> God blesses those whose hearts are pure, for they will see God.
>
> —Matthew 5:8 (NLT)

Not having sex is about learning self-control. You don't really have to have self-control, but if you don't, you just won't have good relationships . . . ever. The reason for practicing self-control is actually love. Dr. Henry Cloud says that the abilities to delay self-gratification and exhibit self-control are prerequisites to the ability to love.[3] Your desires are real, but you can control them. Really. And this becomes important when you think about how casual the topic of sex has become.

Casual Sex Is Not Casual at All

Sex will never be as simple for humans as it is for the dog next door to me who seems to go after anything he can mount. People might treat it casually, but they are fooling themselves, other people, or both. Sex affects people, and people are not casual. Sex changes their outlook, self-worth, and perspective on love. No matter how much people try to make it seem casual in commercials, books, porn, magazines, or in the punch lines of jokes, it's just not. Don't buy into something that is simply and obviously not true.

Touching, Timing, and Pulling Triggers

The desire and act of taking your clothes off and having sex with someone, even your beloved boyfriend or girlfriend, does not just happen. It requires a trigger, and you can control whether or not that trigger is pulled. Both guys and girls have a sex and aggression hormone, and it doesn't just turn on and off immediately, especially for girls. It progresses. It starts with the eyes and moves on. Hands touch, kissing starts, other parts of the body are touched, clothes come off, then touching continues. Usually flirting, kissing, touching, intense kissing, mutual masturbation, oral sex, and outer-course (simulated sex with the penis on the outside of the girl's vagina) all usually happen prior to intercourse. All of these things are progressive, and they each start somewhere. They can be triggered, or they can be avoided.

The likelihood of sexual stuff happening increases when you shut the basement door and get under the covers to watch a movie with no one around. It happens when you drink alcohol. It happens when you say words like "I love you; I want this," which are words that promise closeness and commitment but are meant to arouse the desires of someone else. It happens when people only want to hang out alone all the time, with no one else around.

Here is when this stuff doesn't happen. It doesn't happen if you are considering the best interests of the other person. It doesn't happen if you decide to make some boundaries and rules for yourself and the people you like ahead of time. You are the one who is in control of your switch. Don't let things progress to a place that leaves either one of you regretful.

Even guys don't always love the sex experience. The majority of guys report feeling insecure, and their level of trust and interest in a girl changes once they sleep together. I hope you take comfort in knowing that there are still millions upon millions of teenagers in our country and millions more around the world who are not having sex. In fact, the majority are not. There is no giant-cool-romantic-happy sex party that you are missing out on. People are doing other things too. They are going spelunking, playing basketball, training chimpanzees, reading, laughing, watching a movie, writing a book, doing their homework, talking with a friend, or one of a million other possibilities that include having clothes on and still having fun. Those who jump into something they aren't ready for don't enjoy it. And sex is one thing that is created for enjoyment when it is done right. Oh . . . and babies! Sex makes babies. Don't forget that one. Kind of a big deal.

Remember a Couple of Things

The Bible says something that makes a lot of common sense if we choose to listen to it. In fact, it says the same words three times in the same book. "Do not arouse or awaken love until it so desires" (Song of Solomon 2:7; 3:5; 8:4). This is not simply a rule. Love is a desire, and it progresses. Eventually it shows itself in the physical form. Instead of looking for love and sex, try looking for wisdom. When you do this, love will reveal itself when it is ready.

Kissing Turns Your Head Dumb and to the Right

Did you know that you become a little bit dumb when you kiss? Oh, yeah, and if you kiss, you usually tilt your head to the right. Seriously, about 77.5 percent of people tilt their heads to the right when they lean in for a smooch.[4]

When you kiss someone you like, nerve endings send positive signals to the brain's cortex, and it releases dopamine and endorphins. Dopamine fuels your reward system, and this makes you want to keep kissing. Endorphins, which are natural painkillers, enhance pleasure. Cortisol, a stress hormone, drops when you kiss, and oxytocin, the "hug drug," strengthens the feeling that you are attached to the person.[5]

The endorphins actually make a couple "feel" in love, because their pleasure neurons are all happy. Instead of thinking their way through the relationship, couples can begin to feel their way through the relationship. Too much physical contact usually means their brains and minds are not making decisions anymore—their hormones are guiding them instead. Dangerous. The more physical contact in a relationship, the less the reasoning or rational part of your brain makes the choices about that relationship.

Love Is Actually Patient

My wife still likes me. I'm pretty excited about it too, thank you. I really liked her from the moment I saw her. What I didn't realize was that she was taking notes on me for years. We liked each other, but things weren't really lined up at the time for us to be together. So I was her friend. I'm not saying I haven't made lots and lots of mistakes in my life, but I did do a couple of things right. One of them was that I really just cared about her. I always wanted the best for her. I didn't put on a show for her or try to whisper sweet nothings in her ear. I just listened to her, prayed for her, checked in on her, and demonstrated that I cared. Notice I said demonstrated; I didn't just say things. She noticed that I wasn't being a sleazebag. She noticed that I never pressured her.

And after a long time, when we did start dating, we had already established a really important thing. Trust. She already knew who I was. I had already done the hard work and didn't even know it. Love, care, trust, and sex are all closely interconnected. If you have a waffle brain, then remember that. If you have a spaghetti head, you probably already know this. You can't have great outcomes if you don't have good intentions.

Remember the Dolphins

As a teenager, you have hormones you can't change. It is true that guys and girls will have sexual urges and wonder about sex. It's true that there are a lot of influences on people today regarding their decisions about their sexuality. It is also true that most guys will experience the sudden increase in blood flow to their nether regions from time to time in the hallway or math class, even if they don't love math. And it's true that this will be awkward. But you can still have control of your desires, because you can choose to control how you respond to your urges—and you'll need to.

And sex doesn't start with your body anyway; it starts with your brain. The good news is that you can learn a lot about sex while keeping your pants on. Sex is natural. It is also good. God created sex as a joy, and he did this with us in mind. Whether we choose to make sex incredibly wonderful or incredibly cheap is up to us. Sex is an incredible source of pleasure, but only when understood and treated with care.

For whatever reason God saw fit, dolphins and humans were fortunate enough to be granted access to experience sex in a different way, a beautiful way. Because of this, sex has not only to do with biology and reproduction, but it has just as much to do with the heart and our feelings. A pretty exclusive club when you think about it. We, the people, are a big part of the membership role. So let's try not to mess it up. The dolphins are really counting on us.

FROM BILL AND PAM

Be Epic!

Movies with superheroes almost always seem to be box-office hits. We think that is because deep down, we all have a little desire to be a superhero or to be "epic" in our life. Relationships and how you handle them can be a great place to decide to be epic. But it might feel a bit radical, and it definitely will make you stand out from the crowd— but in a good way.

We (Pam and Bill) come from some pretty chaotic, crazy homes, so we didn't handle dating relationships very well as teens. I (Bill) was a football player at the beginning of high school, so I was part of the popular crowd. Like most of my friends, I made accidental decisions and simply followed my impulses. I was fascinated with a couple of young ladies I dated, but I didn't really know what to do with them. I just followed the girls' lead—whatever that was.

I (Pam) was a cheerleader, and in stereotypical fashion, I was a flirt and a tease. Because of my dad's drinking, I needed the attention of men way too much. I found that I would do almost anything to keep a boyfriend in my life. Neither Bill nor I had a clue what we were doing. After years of frustrating relationships, we decided to do things differently when we met.

Bill's view: Pam was the first girlfriend in my life since I became a Christian. I had no idea how to have a "Christian relationship," so I bought a notebook and started writing down any question I had about how to have a relationship with a girl. Before we could begin a date, I wanted us to talk through the questions I had written down.

Pam's view: I thought the notebook thing was, well, *different*, but Bill was such a great guy—handsome, godly, athletic, and had a great smile—I was willing to go along with the notebook thing because it seemed it was helping us make better choices.

Bill's view: A few of those discussions involved how physical we would be with each other. The day came when it was time to ask if I could kiss Pam. No kidding, this was her response:

"Bill, you are absolutely gorgeous, and I would really like to say yes, but my mentor told me I should ask other couples who have great marriages what they did, and they all waited until they were engaged to kiss. Besides, I haven't done a great job of controlling my desires in the past, and because of that I pretty much wrecked every relationship I had in high school. You see, I read in Matthew 5:8 that the pure in heart will see God, and I want to have a pure heart, and I want you to have a pure heart. Believe me, I looked in the Bible for 'Thou shalt not kiss'—it isn't there! I know it would be okay with God if I kissed you, but like I said, I am not great at controlling my desires, and you are so gorgeous that I just don't know if I could trust myself if I started kissing you. I might want more, and then I might not be able to stop at a kiss. I don't want us to mess up what God is doing in our lives. So, although I really want to say yes, I am going to say no. Is that all right?"

She was cute when she was saying it, but I was stunned. I wasn't upset with her; I was just stunned. I drove her home in silence and told her at the door to her apartment, "I will pick you up for breakfast tomorrow."

Pam's view: Bill responded with complete silence. He drove me home—twenty minutes—in complete silence. I opened the door to my friend's apartment and said, "I might have just lost the very best guy I've ever had in my life!" My friends replied, "What did he do?" I told them the whole story, and they said, "Pam, we have all the read the Bible, and 'Thou shalt not kiss,' it isn't there, but for some weird reason, God asked you to do this, so there must be a reason, because God loves you. Trust God." Then they prayed for me. I stayed up all night praying—for a miracle!

Bill's view: Over breakfast, we began the most significant discussion of our dating relationship. We decided that it would be best for us to not kiss as long as were just dating. People often ask if it were awkward deciding to get engaged before we had kissed. All I can say is, for us, it worked to wait. We have even written a book together called *Red Hot Monogamy*—a book all about how to have passionate love, and our love story has been told around the world in nearly twenty languages! We get to be on TV and radio and tell our love story. That's pretty epic.

Brock and Hannah's Story

So our own sons grew up hearing our love story, and our oldest, somewhere along the way, decided he wanted to be a hero to the woman he would someday marry by saving himself for marriage. One day, I (Pam) was doing a book signing in Phoenix, and I told a story about Brock. The bookstore owner's wife said, "Where did you say Brock got his college scholarship?"

"He's the quarterback at Liberty University," I replied.

"My Hannah is at Liberty!" Then we exchanged pictures and phone numbers of our kids. They dated for eighteen months before Brock asked her parents for their permission to marry Hannah. He had a ring designed and delivered to the football office. The day it arrived, the football secretary called and said, "The eagle has landed." Hannah thought they were just going for fast food, so she had on jeans and a T-shirt that read, "The QB is mine."

Brock took her to the place they first met and handed Hannah a nail. He took her to the place on campus where they had their first deep conversation, and handed her another nail. Then he took her to the chapel where they had first prayed together and handed her a piece of a board. Then he took her off campus, where she was sharing a home with friends, and handed her another board. Then he made a cross out of the nails and the boards and hammered it into the ground. He got down on one knee, opened the ring box, and said, "Hannah, I want our relationship to start at the foot of the cross. Hannah, I love you. Will you marry me? And Hannah, will you kiss me for the first time?" To which Hannah replied, "YES! YES!"

Their love story has now been repeated to millions of people all over the world. Once, Hannah got an e-mail from a friend whose parents are missionaries in China. He was visiting them there and had just heard Brock and Hannah's love story played on the radio in China—now that is EPIC!

You can decide to value your sexuality even after making some mistakes. You can decide now that your sexuality is valuable before you make mistakes. It is never too early or too late to value your sexuality. Your decisions might encourage others to guard their sexuality—and that's epic.

Sin—The Bows and Arrows Kind

I had to teach archery at a camp one summer. I don't know why; I didn't know anything about it. But I learned some basic skills and terms for about four minutes, and then did my best. Mostly, the guys just shot at targets and the occasional squirrel. Some of the terms in archery are strange, at first, like *fletching* and *cockfeather*. But one of them stuck out to me the most: sin. Originally in archery, in ancient Greece, if an archer shot an arrow and missed, a spotter would call out "sin" to let him know he missed the mark and to shoot again. It got me thinking about sin, particularly how I always thought it just meant when I messed up or made a mistake. But now I see it differently. In archery sinning meant missing the intended mark, and that makes a lot more sense for our lives too. People make mistakes. If you are a human being, you know this.

God doesn't want you to follow a list of do's and don'ts. He wants you to hit the mark. He wants you to fulfill a life of worth and meaning. And when we mess things up, we miss out on the plan that he has for us. We miss the intended mark. And we all do. Maybe you have missed the mark when it comes to sex or relationship stuff. Jesus died on the cross so we could be forgiven for all those times, and when we ask him to forgive us, he does, and he helps us make better decisions. Even if you've missed the mark, you can take another shot.

CHAPTER 12

How to Fail at Life

*Failure is not a single, cataclysmic event. You don't
fail overnight. Instead, failure is a few errors in
judgment, repeated every day.*

—Jim Rohn

Fail (v.) 1. To fall short of accomplishing success
or achievement in something, attempted,
desired, or approved. 2. To be unsuccessful in the
performance or completion of a desired outcome.
3. The stuff other people have done plenty of
already so that you won't have to.

This is a chapter about how to fail. My guess and hope is that
you won't read it for advice. I'm going to assume you don't really
want to fail at life or at relationships. It is my sincere desire that
you succeed. And avoiding mistakes that other people make can
be a shortcut to success. You don't have to repeat mistakes that

have already been made. *You don't have to repeat mistakes that have already been made.* Get it?

When you notice a sign in your life that says, "Wrong! This way is a mistake; other people have tried this and failed." I hope you turn around and take a new route. You'll end up having to do it anyway, so why not avoid the negative routes altogether? These topics explain some important signs:

Really? A Wetsuit?

I went through a chubbo phase. I know, it was so great; I really miss it. I was pretty insecure about being chubby, and I seemed to have friends with abnormal amounts of stomach muscles. I went on vacation to a lake with some friends and their parents once. And I brought my wetsuit. It wasn't really cold, but I sure did wear my wetsuit a lot. In fact, I wore it the entire trip whenever we were on the water. It was really hot, and I looked like a total tool. Please, go ahead and imagine a bunch of people lying on a boat, and then picture me lying in a three-quarter-length black wetsuit. I was actually pretty miserable, but I acted like it didn't bother me. I think the girls knew; their spaghetti brains clued them in. But I was

> MacKenzie: I think you should post your chubbo wetsuit photos on your Web site. I think your readers would appreciate it. Really.

> Chad: I'll hop right on that. Thanks for your support.

afraid of people looking at me and thinking any of the one hundred negative thoughts that I thought about myself. I was sweating the entire trip. My fears determined my entire experience. And because of that, my insecurity got bigger, and I enjoyed myself less. And I sweat in large amounts.

Being Afraid

There are all kinds of fears, and we all struggle with them at some point: rejection, inadequacy, abandonment, intimacy, love, loss, and the list goes on. I once heard that courage is simply fear that has said its prayers. I think this is true. It isn't a matter of not having fear in your life; it's a matter of not letting it run your life.

Don't force unhealthy relationships because you're afraid of being alone. Don't try to be someone you're not because you're afraid of what others think. Being a teenager is tough, but it will be easier if you hand over your fears to God.

> MacKenzie: You obviously didn't have this healthy fear when you didn't shower for a month.
>
> Chad: You're right. I had courage . . . and no girlfriend.

There are some good fears, like a healthy fear of bears or of not doing your homework. The fear of smelling really awful might motivate you to take a shower. You should be afraid of smacking your little brother or stealing. But I'm not talking about healthy fears. I'm talking about the deeper fears that keep people from being whole.

A good way to fail is to let fear define your life. So don't. Find the fears in your life that harass you and harass them back. You will be locked in a prison of yourself until you do. And you are not meant to be in a prison. What I mean by harass them is to do the very thing that scares you. Of course, this does not apply to good fears, because those are in your life to protect you. I am talking about dumb fears like the one that inspired my wetsuit solution. I didn't need to think about it about a whole lot, and I didn't need anyone to explain to me all the reasons why a wetsuit was the wrong approach. I needed to just start wearing my bathing suit. If you are afraid of rejection or intimacy, practice your communication skills and start meeting new people with those new skills. If you are afraid of abandonment, start helping others in a positive way.

Guys, Here's a List of Surefire Ways to Get an A+ in Fail.

Pressure People, Especially Girls

If you want to be a stalker/creep/not-fun-person-to-be-around/sexual-assaulter type, then pressure people. Or just don't. Trying to coerce someone to do something that you want is manipulative and usually selfish. Many guys have strong personalities and don't realize they can put pressure on people simply because they are persuasive. Being considerate will serve you much better in life than being selfish and pressuring others.

Embarrass Girls

There is a difference between teasing and embarrassing. No one likes to be embarrassed, especially girls when they are in public. There was a girl hanging out with our crew from a summer bus tour we did. She was really bubbly, and we had a lot of fun with her and her friends. She had a major scar on her body that she was open about, but you could tell it was probably a little hard for her too. She was explaining it in front of everyone when one of her guy friends in the group started to say, "Eww, that is nasty!" Before he could finish speaking, I actually slapped my hand across his mouth so instead he actually said, "Eww, that is naaa—[mouth slapped shut]." I pulled him aside and simply said, "Hey, dude, what you were about to say in front of everyone was going to make her feel ugly or that there was something wrong with her, and it would have embarrassed her a lot. It's probably the equivalent of me getting up on a big stage with a loudspeaker and announcing that you have a really small penis." Then he just looked at me and said, "Oh...dude, that's bad. Okay, I get it now." Girls are sensitive. Make sure that you are being sensitive to them as well.

Don't Listen

My friend Dave is a girl magnet, and he doesn't even try to be. He seems to have a secret skill that girls can't get enough of. He uses the little flaps of skin on the left and right side of his head, his ears. He listens. And I love Dave because of how much he really cares about listening to you. Everyone else loves him too.

> Mackenzie: Are you sure you don't want to explain this whiny thing a little more?
>
> Chad: Yes, I'm sure.

Be the Whiny Guy

Do you really need an explanation?

Be Loud

You are one human being. Don't try to be the voice of everyone. If you do, then everyone will not like you. Give other people room to speak and be heard. Your opinion, though important, is not the most important one.

Be Macho

Strength and confidence aren't an act. Most guys who truly possess these things are actually really nice and comfortable in their own skin. They don't have to prove these things; they just *are* these things. Macho is an act. It may look like it is working for some guys, but a macho persona will not serve you well in the long run.

Be Clingy

Are you constantly sweet-talking girls or clinging to a girl-friend to the point that it takes up more than its fair share of homework time or time with your friends? Then don't. Don't be the clinger. Guys like balance and a little mystery in girls, and girls like the same thing in us as well. Girls can be an important part of your life, but don't mistake them for life itself.

Be Obsessed

If you resemble a high-octane, high-sugar, high-powered energy drink when it comes to your involvement with girls, you might be this guy. He gets too heavy into relationships too quickly. Slow down, there, Turbo. Don't be the little dog in heat, running around looking for something to ... well ... just don't obsess over girls.

Be Johnny Superior

This guy thinks he is somehow superior to girls. Don't be that guy. And especially don't be that guy if your name is

Johnny. When I explain the concept of waffles and spaghetti to teenagers, I ask them which one is better. Most of the time a bunch of guys start screaming, "Waffles! Waffles are awesome; spaghetti sucks!" This is both inaccurate and dumb. Most girls say, "Neither. They're different." Sorry fellas, but that is the correct answer; deal with it. Neither one—and neither gender—is better than the other. So don't treat girls like you're superior.

Put Down People

You can insult people, and you might think you are funny, but eventually you will find yourself home alone because you have no friends. You might be fifteen or you might be forty-five, but you will end up spending most of your time by yourself. The problem with looking down on others is this: when you are looking down on people, you aren't looking up; if you looked up, you would see God. With as many difficulties as people have in life, they don't need more criticism; they need care and love, so give those things to them, not negativity. If you can remember this, you will be happier, have better luck with the ladies, honor God, and be liked more by others.

One-Up and Brag

No one likes someone who has a similar car/hairstyle/girlfriend/boyfriend/vacation story that is just like theirs, only better. It usually impresses exactly zero people.

Be a Player

If you truly want to fail and be miserable, then just start making girls objects. I mean, why not? They are seen mostly as good-looking bodies on magazine covers, eye candy in the backgrounds of movies, accessories for many pro athletes, objects in porn, and maybe even possessions among the guys at your school. Go ahead and do this if you want to experience a mediocre-at-best life, and if you want to be the shallow guy that all the body wash commercials and funny movies tell you that you want to be. I hope you've caught the sarcasm dripping off the page. Commercials are intended to sell you soap and desire, not happiness or fulfillment. I wish that fewer guys would fall prey to this type of outlook. I don't wish those kinds of guys for any girl.

If you don't want to fail in your relationships, then start questioning what it means to value the girls in your life and what type of guy you actually would like to be. Then consider that you are already shaping the type of man that you are becoming. It is simply an accumulation of your habits and decisions over time, and they have already started.

Ladies, Here Are a Few Tips Guaranteed to Bring Failure to a Store Near You.

Swap God for Guys

If you make guys your first priority, if you try to put them in the place in your life where God should be, you will really suffer. They are a disappointing replacement for the real thing, and even the greatest guy will never truly satisfy you. Remember this math equation; God > the sum of guys.

Try to Change Him

Even if you could change a guy, it's not your job. You aren't his mom either, so don't take that role. If people change because of your influence, that's one thing, but to set out to try to change someone is not a great method for good relationships. You can't change him; it's more likely you will change, and probably not for the better.

Get Them to Love You

It's close to impossible to "make" someone like you, let alone "love" you. Love is something you discover and then commit to. There are people in the world who share your values, have interests similar to yours, have characteristics that improve your life, and are very attractive to you. When you commit to someone who is like this, a great relationship can form. If, however, you try to form someone into that person, it will always be up to you to make the relationship work. You cannot force people into these things. Love is not forced; it is freely given. Do not try to fit a round peg in a square hole.

Only Say Yes

If you haven't learned to be comfortable with the word *no*, then you are making your life much more difficult. Making choices simply to please others can make you a pushover who is easily manipulated, pressured, and used. Healthy females don't try to please everyone. You cannot do this anyway. But you can learn how to treat yourself with dignity. Learning to say "no" is a very important part of that. Only saying yes = Fail.

Be Naïve

I wish it were okay to be naïve because it conveys innocence, but the world you live in does not afford you that luxury. Trust is a great thing, but to do it unwisely or before trust is earned is to be naïve. You need to know how to evaluate people, truth, action, and care. Don't just take people at their word. Make them prove it in their actions. Do not be naïve; be informed.

Can you believe that 87 percent of all statistics about dating are made up? No, you can't . . . because you are no longer that naïve.

Date Really Young

There are virtually no benefits to dating young, and the younger you are, the worse the results. People who date young always suffer the most hardships and often wish they would have spent less time on guys and more time on anything else. You cannot have healthy relationships unless you spend time with yourself, your friends, and your family. This takes time. So spend your youth being youthful. TV shows that tell you to be older are stupid.

Constantly Have Boyfriends

Boyfriends are not shoes; you don't always need them. Girls who have to have a boyfriend have more problems than those who don't. They face a much higher risk for depression, emotional pain, poor self-esteem, disease, sexual abuse, and a broken heart. You always need good friends. You don't always need a boyfriend.

Only Focus on the Present

We'll get into this more in the last chapter, but people who use their brain to only focus on the here and now are selling themselves short. You can enjoy the present while thinking about and planning for the future. Enjoy where you are *and* know where you are going, and you won't be thrown off course by the changing tides.

Form Your Identity
Around What You Think Guys Like

Instead of being themselves, these girls fall into the trap of doing exactly the opposite and become a person someone else wants them to be. They will find later that they have to go back and figure themselves out anyway before someone can really appreciate them. Why not make your mold in the image of God instead of what this week's social forecast is telling you? People appreciate you more for being yourself, not what you think they want you to be.

Become the Double Standard

Here's it is: a girl might become sexual with a guy and believe it will make them closer. She might even picture herself married to him. While a guy might choose to be sexually active with a girl, it actually lessens his desire to see her as marriage material. Or as teen guys commonly say, "I wouldn't marry her, but I would totally get it on with her." I know this is confusing, but sadly, you can be led to think that intimacy equals progression in the relationship when, in fact, it does not. Remember that, on average, less than four weeks after teens have sex, they break up. Don't be a victim of the double standard.

Guy Bash

If you don't think that guys should bash girls, then it would be wise to apply the same standard to yourself. While there are some legitimate reasons why girls want to talk badly about guys, it only adds a problem to a problem. If you have an issue with a guy, try talking to him first. You might be surprised to see that guys are willing to learn if approached in a nonthreatening way.

And even if that doesn't work, don't stoop to the level of demeaning him. Guys need to be encouraged, just like girls. This leaves no room for guy bashing.

BILL AND PAM

Karate or Karaaazy?

Trust us, there are a few things girls do that make guys run the other direction. Here are some we have seen from our years in youth ministry and from the lives of our own sons and their friends. A guy will think you are crazy and want to run if you:

- Tuck in his shirt, pick out his clothes, tell him how to wear his hair, or do other "mom-like" actions.
- Yell at him, slap him, or throw stuff at him.
- Lock yourself in his car, room, or dorm room until he gets back together with you.
- Tell him to quit sports, quit his job, skip class, or ignore homework because "you don't have enough time for me."
- Make fun of him in front of his friends.
- Play games and pit him against his friends or family to somehow "prove his love" for you.
- Constantly compare him to other guys and list off ways they are better than he is.

- Pressure him to have sex, or manipulate him into doing things he doesn't want to do or isn't ready for.
- Nag him to do mean things to past girlfriends.
- Make fun of his mom or dad. Even if he has bad parents, he doesn't need you to mock them. It is okay to agree with him and sympathize with him, but be careful not to cross over to ridicule, outright hatred, or disrespect.

While you will make mistakes, others have already made plenty for you. You can learn from them, and by doing so, you can avoid some frustration and heartache. After all, there is a lot of wisdom in the old saying, "Those who cannot learn from history are doomed to repeat it." I hope you don't have to repeat it. It's probably better that you just go and enjoy your day.

CHAPTER 13

Your Brain Doesn't Work . . . Completely

I went for a walk last night and my kids asked me how long I was going to be gone. I said, "The whole time."

—STEVEN WRIGHT

When I was a teenager and even for a few years after my adolescence, I did all kinds of awesome things. And by awesome I mean dumb. I have always really enjoyed doing physically exhilarating things. The day I was old enough to jump out of an airplane, I was ecstatic with joy. By 9:00 a.m. I was signed up and sitting on an airstrip with a parachute on my back, and I was really, really excited to throw myself out of a plane for my eighteenth birthday.

In Alaska and in some other wilderness settings, I have done a number of things that easily could have shortened my life span. My friend dared me to walk out into the middle of a herd of wild buffalo. I did. Instantly I realized what a horrible decision that was.

When I led a kayak trip (also in Alaska), I paddled over to a school of sharks, which I then discovered was feeding. While I was in the middle of about fifty or sixty sharks, one of them started swimming alongside my kayak, and something in my brain told me that I should touch it. I did. Again, this was a horrible decision. The shark slammed into my kayak and nearly tipped me over. I cried.

My friend and I decided to play chicken with Jet Skis, but neither of us was smart enough to chicken out. Turns out Jet Skis are really expensive.

A good friend of mine told me that there was no way I could stand on top of a six-inch railing on a hundred-foot bridge and pee off of it. And by now you get the point.

As a young person, I did a lot of things that were unsafe or otherwise lacked good judgment. But most of them were before I was about twenty-four or twenty-five. The weird part is that they never seemed like bad ideas at the time. It turns out my brain wasn't working . . . completely, and neither does yours. My brain works now, I'm pretty sure. I instantly see the risk of things more often. While this cuts down on the amount of cool stories about me potentially dying, I actually break bones less often, and I seem to have fewer medical bills. So let me say this to you:

Your brain is not yet developed! Or at least one very crucial part isn't.

It doesn't matter whether you are a guy or a girl. Your brain is not fully developed. You know when you're riding in a car with a friend, and he is blaring the radio while driving really fast and weaving in and out of lanes, all while talking to his friends in the car and texting? That's actually the lack of the brain-development thing. And what science, insurance rates, and our relationships tell us is that your brain will keep developing until you are about twenty-five. You know, right when you get that final discounted driver rate. By the way, those rates are calculated very carefully.

Point at Your Brain

You know how teachers poke you in the forehead and say, "Use your head!"? Well, first of all, that's annoying. Second, and more important, this is the part of your head that contains the frontal lobe, and it does not fully mature while you are a teenager. This has huge implications for you. The frontal lobe contains most of the dopamine-sensitive neurons, which are associated with reward, attention, long-term memory, planning, and drive or motivation.

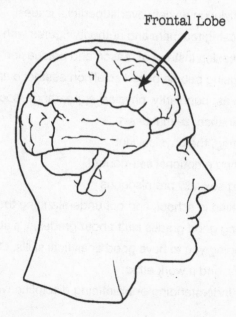

Frontal Lobe

The primary function of the frontal lobe involves the ability to recognize future consequences based on current actions, to choose between good and bad actions, to control unacceptable social and emotional responses, and to recognize similarities and differences between things. The frontal lobe is involved in higher mental functions. These are all the things I was not demonstrating when my hand was outstretched, trying to grab a shark fin as I sat in a small kayak. The underdeveloped frontal lobe is also demonstrated in all kinds of other ways in teens:

- Driving recklessly
- Obsessing about one high school relationship, then the next one, then the next one . . .
- Becoming too clingy and committed
- Surrounding yourself with constant social drama and living in anxiety over superficial issues
- Opposing teachers and authority figures with aggression instead of reason and persuasion
- Choosing people based solely on aesthetic appeals such as: popularity, physical appearance, social dominance, sexual desire
- Fighting, the physical kind
- Lacking emotional self-control
- Being sexually promiscuous
- Slacking in school, and not understanding that getting good grades isn't about grades, it's about prepping you to have good analytical skills, ethical views, and a work ethic
- Not understanding or practicing discipline with

boundaries. (*Boundaries* are commonly mistaken
as rules to keep you from doing things. They're
not. FYI.)

- Texting, sexting, and compromising physical, verbal,
and emotional boundaries
- Eating whatever you want because it hasn't made
you too fat or unhealthy yet
- Not understanding that the pictures you are taking
of yourself and sending might end up on the Internet
- Not understanding that the World Wide Web goes
beyond the computer in your room, and is actually,
in fact, *World Wide*

However, just because thinking about future consequences does not come naturally, it doesn't mean you are not capable of doing it. You are, in fact, in control of these decisions. You can override your limited prefrontal abilities. In fact, even small children are capable of realizing that reckless driving and shark touching are not good decisions.

Back to Waffles and Spaghetti

We've discussed that guys and girls are extremely different, and often, this seems most obvious in relationships. One of the reasons why you guys don't understand girls, and you girls don't understand guys, is because your brain is still learning how to figure these things out. And it will be doing this for quite a while still, so don't rush it or your brain will get mad at you. When people try to force, push, or simply hope for others to be at a place in their development where they are not, they are asking the brain to do things that it does not do well. Here are some questions that are better answered when your brain develops more:

- Why don't guys care about relationships?
- How come girls talk so much?
- Are guys just thinking about sex all the time?
- Why do girls make a big deal out of so many things?

In time, and hopefully after this book, many of these questions will not seem as difficult as they once did. When the frontal lobe develops, people care more deeply about having long-term, trusting, and healthy serious relationships. They also know more about what they actually need in the person they are with and in the relationship itself. They simply have better judgment because the judgment part of their brain works better.

My Broom Taught Me About Life

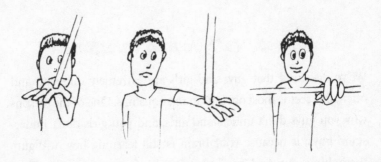

Here is something that I do a lot with teens: take a broomstick and balance it in the palm of your hand. Now, the first time you try this, only stare at the bottom of the broomstick handle. I mean, put your face really close into it and only focus on the first one or two inches. Try to balance it. How did it go? Whenever I do this with guys, they can't do it and sometimes get mad thinking I'm trying to trick them. It's kind of funny. Guys are sensitive. Girls don't take this so personally as a judgment of their athletic ability. Now, the second time you try to balance the stick, back your face away and focus on the entire broomstick, particularly the top of it. You will notice immediately that it is much easier to balance, and almost anyone can do it. If you can't, sorry. Just try to get the point by reading, I guess. What's remarkable is that when I ask the students which time they were trying harder to balance the broomstick, they say the first time. They were intensely focused, but they still couldn't do it. And if effort isn't the key to success, then what is? It turns out it's something else. Perspective. You don't change the amount of effort; you change your perspective, and it changes the outcome. Now take the broomstick or broomstick-type object, and turn it sideways. This no longer represents a broomstick. It now represents time. It represents the timeline of your life. If you focus on only the tiny portion you are experiencing at this very second or this very week, your broomstick will probably fall a lot, or at least will wobble back and forth too much.

If you can learn to focus beyond the immediate present and look and plan for things you want later in life, things you like, experiences you want to have, places you want to see; if you think about your hopes, dreams, plans, and future relationships, then you will find that you can more easily enjoy the present, and you can balance your broomstick much more easily. Your perspective changes your outlook, and your outlook changes your actions.

Write It Down

Asking you to change your perspective requires you to use your frontal lobe, and while you do use this region, it's not a natural thing for your brain. But thinking about the future makes you use this part of the brain. And doing this helps you.

Write down your goals. When you write things, you solidify them more easily as a memory. You'll also make yourself think about things that you want. This, in turn, will help your mind process these things.

Write down some dreams you have for the next ten years of your life in the following categories:

Romance

Do you want to get married? If yes, at what age?

_____

_____

_____

What traits are you now attracted to in the opposite sex? Are these traits you'd like to live with for the rest of your life?

_____

_____

_____

What kind of person do you want to marry? Describe.

_____

_____

_____

What would you like to do before you get married?

_____

_____

_____

Travel

Do you like to travel? What are some of your favorite places
to visit?

_____

_____

_____

What places would you like to see in your lifetime? Which of these
would you like to see in the next ten years? Why?

_____

_____

_____

Do you want to move to a new place? Where is it? Why would you
like living there?

_____

_____

_____

Adventures

Are you an adventurous person?

_____

_____

_____

What types of adventures do you want to have?

_____

_____

_____

_____

When do you want to have them?

_____

_____

_____

_____

Education and Career

What educational goals do you have for yourself? How much schooling do you want to get?

_____

_____

_____

What are your interests? What do you want to study?

_____

_____

_____

_____

What do you want your career to be? What do you need to do to accomplish that?

_____

_____

_____

What books do you want to read?

_____

_____

_____

If you could be anything and money didn't matter, what would you be?

_____

_____

_____

When I was a teenager, I used to write down all of the places that I wanted to see. I drew places that I found in magazines: a cove off the coast of Spain, with a sunken ship; a forest in Germany; the Amazon River in South America; Mount McKinley in Alaska; Mount Everest in Tibet; the Congo in Africa; Machu Picchu in Peru; Teahupo'o in Tahiti; and all fifty states. And when I did that, it made me more likely to make those dreams come true. I have already traveled to a few of the exotic places on my list, and I have added about three hundred more to a new list. When you think about the future, you exercise your brain. You force yourself to look farther down the timeline of your life and will not be stuck thinking only about the moment you are in. And this brings me to another point . . .

Let Them Change!

Here is a pretty simple thing to remember about yourself and other people: you are going to change! You, both guys and girls, are not done developing. You are going to change dramatically, and I'm not just talking about the amount of armpit hair guys develop. You will change in almost every life category.

Meet My Meathead Friends

I had some rather jock, muscle-head friends in high school. There were several whose personalities resembled the most meathead, tough-guy, football-loving, partying, drinking, fighting, womanizing, chauvinistic guys that you could find. Many of these guys were all-state and nationally ranked football players. And people admired them for it. A lot of them were jerks to people from other schools, other guys and girls. Sometimes they were so concerned about being known for being awesome themselves that they forgot to make other people feel awesome. But something strange happened to a couple of them. High school ended and, even if they played football in college, people didn't really like them. No one cared how big they were; people cared if they were being respectful instead of rude. They learned a simple truth. People like others who are genuine and who are interested in other people. No one likes a self-centered person for very long.

If you met some of these guys today, you would be shocked. They are some of the nicest guys ever. They are kind, considerate, funny, and genuine. They learned from experience how to treat others. While not everyone will change, many people will. And the way people seem today will probably look dramatically different three years from now, and two years after that, and four years after that. A couple of these guys are pretty embarrassed by how they acted when they were younger. I know; I try to remind them of it on a regular basis. Unfortunately for me, they still remember how to punch.

Give people some breathing room. It doesn't mean that you have to date them, accept bad behavior, wait around for change, or really do anything at all. Just don't stamp and seal people in a box. Give them time and room to grow out of it. I'm sure you hope they'll do the same for you.

Turtles and Rabbits

I tried to sprint a mile once. I don't know why I decided to, I just did. I got just past a lap and a half when I fell to my knees and threw up everywhere. Turns out the world-record holder in the mile run trained pretty hard to build up to his mile-sprinting ability. No one has ever asked for my advice on running since. But then again, they never really did before either. If you visit Boston, Massachusetts, and go to Copley Square (the finish line for the Boston Marathon), you'll see a peculiar statue. It's a statue of a turtle and a rabbit, and it represents the old tale of the tortoise and the hare. As you probably remember, the tortoise was ridiculed by the hare because he moved too slowly. In return the tortoise challenged the mocking hare to a race. So sure of himself, the hare dashed out ahead and left the tortoise out of sight. The hare became winded, bored, and so self-assured that he took a break. He sat under a tree and fell asleep. As he slept, the tortoise passed him and slowly but surely made his way to the finish line and beat the rabbit. And of course the story illustrates a simple moral. Slow and steady usually wins the race.

If their story applies to young people, it applies this way:

Don't sprint everywhere. Find the pace that is best for you and live it. Don't be in such a hurry, don't be so frantic, and don't make fun of small animals. You aren't missing anything. If you rush by one thing in an attempt to get to the other, you miss the scenery along the way. It takes a long time to gain understanding of yourself and other people.

Everywhere I have been, teenagers seem to be in such a hurry to get someplace in their lives that they can't yet be. They seem to be in a hurry to experience romantic relationships, sex, certain movies or hobbies, and a bunch of other stuff that they aren't ready for. You cannot really experience these things very well right now, no matter how much you try. But you will get there. Some kids get criticized for being slower to grow up, timid, old-fashioned, too religious, or inexperienced. One: So what? Who cares? It's okay to be these things. Two: Maybe some people just go at a different pace. Maybe the paced people actually have something figured out that the sprinters don't. What I do know is that nobody can sprint all the time.

Slow and steady is a pretty good way to take in things more fully. You'll need that experience and information, and there's a lot of it to soak up. When you hurry, you miss stuff. Good stuff. Take your time; enjoy the journey.

Waffles and Spaghetti—Final Thought

It's amazing how much guys and girls have in common. It's equally amazing how different we are from one another.

If you are a waffle, you will spend your entire life trying to figure out spaghetti. You will always wonder why girls do things that seem so foreign to you. You will always be a little baffled by why they need to talk so much, express their emotions in larger amounts and more frequently, and you might be slightly frightened when you see them both laughing and crying at the same time. Because, after all, how in the world can someone combine these two things at the same time?

If you are spaghetti, you will still always be wondering about the waffle. You will wonder why guys seem to put everything in life into neat little boxes. You will be perplexed at the way they close themselves off. You will wonder if they have any feelings, since they don't like to talk about them. You will also be confused by the amount of scratching, itching, flicking, punching, burping, farting, and other "expressive" forms of art guys do.

And here is the point: you might understand some things about the opposite sex. You might even learn and figure out a lot of things. Hopefully this book helps! But you'll never understand the opposing sex completely. You cannot experience the things they do.

But you can value people. You can do this even with people who don't speak your language. You can do this with almost anyone. You can do this with people you don't even like that much. You can do this if you're athletic, nerdy, pretty, smart, not-so-smart, funny, mathematical, artsy, earthy, or a normal, everyday teenager. You don't have to completely understand everything to love people.

People prefer love and acceptance, and the world needs more of it. And God smiles on it. I hope you will find the joy in it. I hope you will enjoy each other.

Accept one another, then, just as Christ accepted you, in order to bring praise to God.

—ROMANS 15:7

Study Guide

Chapter 1

1. What do you think are some of the best things about being the gender you are?

_____

_____

What does Psalms 139:13–14 say about the way God made each of us?

> For you created my inmost being;
>   you knit me together in my mother's womb.
> I praise you because I am fearfully and wonderfully made;
>   your works are wonderful,
>   I know that full well.

2. What are the things you find most intriguing about the opposite sex?

_____

_____

3. What are the things you find most frustrating about the opposite sex?

_____

_____

4. Have you ever gone twenty-eight days without showering? Explain.

_____

_____

Chapter 2

1. In what ways have you seen guys in your life demonstrate waffle traits?

_____

_____

2. In what ways have you seen girls in your life demonstrate spaghetti traits?

_____

_____

3. How do you feel about miniature horses? Are they a great animal or the greatest animal?

_____

4. What do you think are some potential problems that can arise if guys and girls do not make efforts to understand each other and communicate effectively?

_____

_____

5. How can following 1 Timothy 4:12 help us to have better relationships?

Don't let anyone look down on you because you are young, but set an example for the believers in speech, in life, in love, in faith and in purity.

_____

_____

Since it is God who made us this way, what do you think are some good or beneficial things that can come out of our differences?

_____

_____

Chapter 3

1. Have you ever thought about how much your biology affects you? If so, how?

_____

_____

2. In what ways are you like your mom? In what ways are you like your dad? Which of these things do you think are because of biology, and which are because of learned behaviors?

_____

_____

What do fathers do according to 1 Thessalonians 2:9–12?

_____

_____

What do mothers do according to 1 Thessalonians 2:7–8?

_____

_____

3. Point to your thalamus. Point to someone else's. Are they looking at you funny? Good.

4. What biological differences do you obviously display that are typical for your gender? Which are a little more unusual?

_____

_____

Chapter 4

For the Girls

1. Can you relate to Nicole's story at the beginning of the chapter? Are there times you find yourself overwhelmed and crying, sometimes even when you can't pinpoint the problem?

_____

_____

2. Have you ever compared yourself to Eve? Which good traits of hers do you share? Which negative ones do you share?

_____

_____

3. Is it easy or hard for you to be yourself around others, particularly guys? Why?

_____

_____

4. Do you put pressure on guys or other people to make you feel complete? In what ways?

_____

_____

5. List five great things about yourself.

_____

_____

_____

_____

For the Guys

1. Did you learn anything new about girls in this chapter?

_____

_____

2. After reading this, what are some things you think will help you as you relate to girls?

_____

_____

_____

For Everyone:

1. According to Matthew 5:8 what is the most important part of your life? Why?

Blessed are the pure in heart, for they will see God.

_____

_____

Chapter 5

For the Guys

1. What's your favorite "guy" thing to do with your buddies? Why?

_____

_____

_____

2. What things do you struggle with that Adam did not before "The Fall?" Girls, anger, ego, or risk? In what ways do you struggle?

_____

_____

3. Have you ever had a humiliating experience that was a major blow to your confidence? How did you deal with it? Can you laugh about it yet? How about now?

_____

_____

_____

4. How do you think Leonidas got the forty-six-pack abs? Does this question make you feel uncomfortable? Does it make Leonidas?

_____

_____

5. List five great things about yourself. Now add one more.

_____

_____

_____

_____

For the Girls

1. What did you learn about guys in this chapter that you didn't already know?

_____

_____

2. Is there something in this chapter that will help you have a better understanding of the guys in your life?

_____

_____

For Everyone:

1. How can living out Romans 13:12b–14 help you be a better person?

So let us put aside the deeds of darkness and put on the armor of light. Let us behave decently, as in the daytime, not in orgies and drunkenness, not in sexual immorality and debauchery, not in dissension and jealousy. Rather, clothe yourselves with the Lord Jesus Christ, and do not think about how to gratify the desires of the sinful nature.

_____

_____

Chapter 6

1. Before reading this chapter, were you aware of how much your body was talking?

_____

_____

2. What negative nonverbal habits do you have? Which positive ones do you have?

_____

_____

3. What kind of people do you tend to attract? Do you think this is related to your communication habits or a nonverbal cue such as the way you dress?

_____

_____

_____

4. An-cay ou-yay peak-say ig-pay atin-lay? Awesome. Me too.

5. What are five things you can do to improve your nonverbal communication? (Think about all aspects, body language, clothing, hygiene, posture, tone of voice, and responding to others.)

_____

_____

_____

_____

_____

Chapter 7

1. Think of a good experience you've had talking with the opposite sex. What made it good?

_____

_____

_____

2. Now think of a frustrating experience you've had. What made it bad?

_____

_____

3. Do you think Jordan's "talent" will affect his ability to obtain a girlfriend? Why or why not? Spend less than one minute on this.

_____

_____

4. How often do you text? Are there times you text when you really should call? Have you or your friends gotten caught up in sexting? What boundaries do you need to set to protect yourself?

_____

_____

5. What skill do you need to work on to "talk more better" with members of the opposite sex? How do you think this will help?

_____

_____

6. What is the goal of communication in Ephesians 4:29?

Do not let any unwholesome talk come out of your mouths, but only what is helpful for building others up according to their needs, that it may benefit those who listen.

_____

_____

Chapter 8

1. How many people have you dated, and at what age did you start dating? If you haven't, what are some of the reasons you are waiting?

_____

_____

_____

2. When you are twenty-five, how do you think you'll look back on your current dating choices?

_____

_____

_____

3. What does God say in 2 Samuel 16:7 about the kind of people we should hang around?

> But the LORD said to Samuel, "Do not consider his appearance or his height, for I have rejected him. The LORD does not look at the things man looks at. Man looks at the outward appearance, but the LORD looks at the heart."

_____

_____

_____

4. What are the pros and cons of dating or not dating in high school?

_____

_____

_____

5. Do you know what an algorithm is? Explain. Try not look it up on the Internet first.

_____

_____

6. Describe some characteristics of your ideal dating relationship. What does that look like? If you're in a relationship, does it match up?

_____

_____

Chapter 9

1. Do you feel ready to date? Why or why not?

_____

2. In the list of dating "stop signs" are there any you have struggled with? Which ones? What have you done or what can you do to get help?

_____

_____

3. What type of people should we consider dating and not dating in 2 Corinthians 6:14?

Do not be yoked together with unbelievers. For what do righteousness and wickedness have in common? Or what fellowship can light have with darkness?

_____

_____

_____

4. What is your favorite idea for a date that you have been on or that you would like to go on? (And, have you fed ducks on a date? Or been to Disneyland?)

_____

_____

5. Referring back your list of things you will never do on a date, when do you think you should set up these boundaries—before or after you've begun a relationship? Why?

_____

_____

6. Have you had a positive high school dating relationship that has been spiritually, physically, and emotionally healthy?

_____

_____

Chapter 10

1. Would you say you have a lot or little conflict in your life? Would you attribute its presence or absence to yourself or to those around you?

_____

_____

2. In the list of tips to handle conflict, which do you use well? Which do you need to work on?

_____

_____

3. What things consist of your "giant button?" How can you learn to control them?

_____

_____

_____

4. Are you aggressive, passive, or assertive?

_____

_____

5. Romans 12:18 says: "If it is possible, as far as it depends on you, live at peace with everyone." How does this affect the way you interact with others?

_____

_____

Chapter 11

1. Are you surprised to find out how differently guys and girls think about sex? If so, why? If not, how did you become aware of this?

_____

_____

2. The Bible tells us to avoid sexual immorality in 1 Corinthians 6:18:

Flee from sexual immorality. All other sins a man commits are outside his body, but he who sins sexually sins against his own body.

Before reading this chapter, have you ever thought of this as a principle as opposed to a rule? Knowing that it is meant to protect and not restrain you, how does that affect you?

_____

_____

3. What sexual choices have you made? What have been the benefits or consequences of those decisions? How will they affect you in five years? Ten years? Three minutes?

_____

_____

4. Look back at the chart on page 161. Where is the best place on the chart for a person to set boundaries so that they are treating themselves and others with high value?

_____

_____

5. Will you ever be able to think of dolphins the same? Explain.

_____

_____

_____

Chapter 12

1. What's your definition of failure?

_____

_____

_____

2. Are you doing anything right now that may cause you to fail? Are you doing anything that will cause you to succeed?

_____

_____

3. How is God involved in our failures according to Jeremiah 29:11?

For I know the plans I have for you," declares the Lord, *"plans to prosper you and not to harm you, plans to give you hope and a future."*

_____

_____

4. Have you ever worn a wetsuit when it was insanely hot outside or done something similarly ridiculous out of fear?

_____

_____

5. In the list of ways to fail, are there any you do? What can you do to stop?

_____

_____

Chapter 13

1. Would you touch a shark fin? Explain the circumstances. (Not recommended. Ever.)

2. What are some things you or your friends have done that lacked good judgment?

3. What are some ways to safeguard yourself from making poor decisions in the future? What is one of the keys to making good decisions in 1 Corinthians 15:33?

   Do not be misled: "Bad company corrupts good character."

4. What things do you most want God to help you with right now? Decisions, relationships, your future, or circumstances out of your control? Write out a prayer listing everything you can think of and thank him for being in control.

5. What are some ways guys and girls are alike? And what's your favorite thing about how different we are?

Acknowledgments

For all the weird conversations it took to get this book finished, and for putting up with me, a special thanks to MacKenzie and Laura M.

Thank you very much, Bill and Pam. Co-authoring sounded scary, but you made it a great experience. And thanks for your clever, edible concept.

—CHAD

To Chad and MacKenzie, thanks for making *Men Are Like Waffles, Women Are Like Spaghetti* relevant to the next generation. To Bob Hawkins and the Harvest House team, thanks for having a vision to get great information into the hands of those under twenty-one. May God bless you for your generosity. To Lee Hough, thanks for co-coordinating so many people for such a worthy project. To our new Thomas Nelson Family, thanks for welcoming us into the fold. With great appreciation, "I thank my God every time I remember you." —Philippians 1:3

—PAM AND BILL FARREL

Notes

Chapter 2

1. Paul Coughlin, *Married but Not Engaged* . . . (Bloomington, MN: Bethany House Publishers, 2006), 98–99.

Chapter 3

1. James Dobson, *Bringing Up Boys* (Wheaton, IL: Tyndale, 2005), 16.

2. Melissa Hines, *Brain Gender* (New York, NY Oxford University Press, 2004), 21–25.

3. Ibid.

4. Willy Pedersen, Lars Wichstrøm, and Morten Blekesaune, "Violent Behaviors, Violent Victimization, and Doping Agents: A Normal Population Study of Adolescents," *Journal of Interpersonal Violence* 16 (2001): 806–33.

5. J. Brebner, "Gender and Emotions," *Personality and Individual Differences* 34, no. 3 (February 2006): 387–94; Renato M. E. Sabbatini, "Neurons and Synapses: The History of Its Discovery," *Brain & Mind* 17 (April–July 2003); T. H. Bennett, et. al, "The Neuron Doctrine, Redux," *Science* 310, no. 5749 (November 4, 2005): 791–93.

6. Eric. H. Chudler, "Brain Facts and Figures," http://faculty.washington. edu/chudler/facts.html; A. Dubb, et. al, "Characterization of Sexual Dimorphism in the Human Corpus Callosum," *Neuroimage* 20, no. 1 (September 2003): 512–19.

7. K. M. Bishop and D. Wahsten, "Sex Differences in the Human Corpus Callosum: Myth or Reality?" *Neuroscience and Behavioral Reviews* 21, no. 5 (September 1997): 581–601.

8. Louan Brizendine, *The Female Brain* (New York: Broadway Books, 2006): 53–71.

9. Kristin Cobb, "His-and-Her Hunger Pangs: Gender Affects the Brain's Response to Food," *Science News* 162, no. 1 (July 6, 2002): 4.

10. Marilyn Elias *"Decades of Details Flood Woman with Unmatched Memory," USA Today*, May 6, 2008, http://www.usatoday.com/news/ health/2008-05-07-cant-forget-price_N.htm.

11. Hines, *Brain Gender*, 112–22; Bill Farrel and Pam Farrel, *Why Men and Women Act the Way They Do* (Eugene, OR: Harvest House Publishers, 2003), 39.

12. Jennifer Warner, "Scream for a Healthy Heart," *WebMD Medical News*, November 6, 2002, my.webmd.com/content/article/60/67095.htm.

13. Theresa M. Glomb, "Workplace Anger and Aggression: Informing Conceptual Models with Data from Specific Encounters," *Journal of Occupational Health Psychology* 7, no. 1 (January 2002): 20–36.

Chapter 4

1. Tasia Young and Mary B. Harris, "Most Admired Women and Men: Gallup, Good Housekeeping, and Gender," *Sex Roles: A Journal of Research* 35 (1996): 363–74.

2. Hines, *Brain Gender*, 18–19.

3. Ibid., 109–11.

4. Arthur P. Arnold, "Sex Chromosomes and Brain Gender," *Nature Reviews: Neuroscience* 5, no. 9 (September 2004): 701–8.

Chapter 5

1. Jon Krakauer, *Into the Wild* (New York: Anchor Books, 1996), 127.

Chapter 6

1. B. C. Jones, L. M DeBruine, and A. C. Little, "Integrating Gaze Direction and Expression in Preferences for Attractive Faces," *Psychological Science* 17, no.7, http://www.faceresearch.org/students/ papers/Jones_2006.pdf; Christopher K. Hsee; Elaine Hatfield, and Claude Chemtob, "Assessments of the Emotional States of Others: Conscious Judgments Versus Emotional Contagion," *Journal of Social and Clinical Psychology* 11 (1992):119–28; Peter A. Andersen, *Nonverbal Communication: Forms and Functions*, 2nd ed. (Long Wave, IL: Waveland Press, 2007).

2. Andersen, *Nonverbal Communication*; Barbara and Allen Pease, *The Definitive Book of Body Language* (New York: Bantam Publishers, 2006), 131–192.

3. Norbert Mesko and Tamas Bereczkei, "Hairstyle as an Adaptive Means of Displaying Phenotypic Quality," *Human Nature* 15, no. 3 (2004): 251–70, http://www.evolutionpsychology.com/hair1.pdf.

4. *Wikipedia*, s.v. "Pheromone," http://en.wikipedia.org/wiki/Pheromone; P. Karlson and M. Lüscher, "Pheromones: a New Term for a Class of Biologically Active Substances," *Nature* 183 (January 3, 1959): 55–56. Bear, Mark F.; Barry W. Connors, Michael A. Paradiso (2006).

5. G. P. Williams and C. L. Kleinke, "Effects of Mutual Gaze and Touch on Attraction, Mood, and Cardiovascular Activity," *J Res Pers* 24:145–61.

6. Judith A. Hall, Jason D. Carter, and Terrence G. Horgan, "Gender Differences in Nonverbal Communication of Emotion," in Agneta H. Fischer, ed., *Gender and Emotion: Social Psychological Perspectives* (Cambridge, UK: Cambridge University Press, 2000), 97–117.

7. Sharon Livingston and Glen Livingston, *How to Use Body Language* (Windham, NH: Psy Tech Publishing Inc., 2004).

8. Lee Ann Renninger, T. Joel Wade, and Karl Grammer, "Getting That Female Glance: Patterns and Consequences of Male Nonverbal Behavior in Courtship Contexts," *Evolution and Human Behavior* 25: 416–31.

9. Andersen, *Nonverbal Communication*, 250–259.

10. Jones, DeBruine, and. Little, "Integrating Gaze Direction," 588–91.

11. Nicholas Guéguen, "Courtship Compliance: The Effect of Touch on Women's Behavior," *Social Influence* 2, issue 2 (June 2007): 81–97; Jena Pincott, *Do Gentleman Really Prefer Blondes?* (New York: Bantam Dell, 2008), 156–84.

Chapter 7

1. Fiona Macrae, "Women Talk Three Times as Much as Men, Says Study," November 2006, http://www.dailymail.co.uk/femail/article-419040/Women-talk-times-men-says-study.html; Douglas D. Burman, Tali Bitan, and James R. Booth, "Sex Differences in Neural Processing of Language Among Children," *Neuropsychologia* 46, issue 5 (April 2008): 1349–62, http://www.sciencedirect.com/science?_ob=ArticleURL&_udi=B6T0D-4RH951P-1&_user=10&_rdoc=1&_fmt=&_orig=search&_sort=d&view=c&_acct=C000050221&_version=1&_urlVersion=0&_userid=10&md5=576f8d3ee6dbce4f65db8e1db10ef6ec.

2. Richard F Thompson, *The Brain: An Introduction to Neuroscience* (New York: Worth Publishers, 2000).

3. Judy Rose, "*The 25 Funniest Analogies (Collected by High School English Teachers*," 2006, http://writingenglish.wordpress.com/2006/09/12/the-25-funniest-analogies-collected-by-high-school-english-teachers/.

4. The National Campaign to Prevent Teen and Unplanned Pregnancy, *Sex and Tech: Results from a Survey of Teens and Young Adults* (2009), http://www.thenationalcampaign.org/sextech/PDF/SexTech_Summary.pdf.

5. John Gottman, *Why Marriages Succeed or Fail: And How You Can Make Yours Last* (New York: Fireside, 1994, 1995), 29, 57.

Chapter 8

1. Martha L. Munson and Paul D. Sutton, "Births, Marriages, Divorces, and Deaths: Provisional Data for 2005," *National Vital Statistics Reports* 53, no. 21 (2006).

2. Divorce Rates, http://www.divorceform.org/rates.html.

3. Robert E. Rector, et. al, *The Harmful Effects of Early Sexual Activity and Multiple Sexual Partners Among Women: A Book of Charts* (Washington, D.C.: The Heritage Foundation, June 26, 2003), http://www.heritage.org/research/abstinence/abstinence_charts.cfm; Centers for Disease Control and Prevention, National Center for Health and Statistics, Division of Vital Statistics, various years, http://www.cdc.gov/; Arthur Aron, et. al, "Reward, Motivation, and Emotion Systems Associated with Early-Stage Intense Romantic Love," *Journal of Neurophysiology* 94 (2005): 327–37.

4. Pincott, *Do Gentleman Really Prefer Blondes?*, 281–83.

5. J. Simao and P. M. Todd, "Emergent Patterns of Mate Choice in Human Populations," *Artificial Life* 9, issue (Fall 2003): 403–17.

6. P. M. Todd, "Coevolved Cognitive Mechanisms in Mate Search: Making Decisions in a Decision-Shaped World," in Joseph P. Forgas, Martie G. Haselton, and William von Hippel, eds., *Evolution and the Social Mind: Evolutionary Psychology and Social Cognition* (New York: Psychology Press, 2007), 147–58.

Chapter 9

1. U.S. Department of Justice, "Sexual Assault of Young Children as Reported to Law Enforcement: Victim, Incident, and Offender Characteristics: Statistics, 2006."

2. http://www.cdc.gov/nchs/, various years and articles.

Chapter 10

1. Susan Carney, "Conflict Resolution Styles: Approaches to Interpersonal Problem Solving for Teens," February 14, 2008, Suite101.com, http://youthdevelopment.suite101.com/article.cfm/conflict_resolution_styles#ixzz09Y2xmrUN.

2. Bill Farrel and Pam Farrel, *Men Are Like Waffles—Women Are Like Spaghetti: Understanding and Delighting in Your Differences* (Eugene, OR: Harvest House, 2001), chap. 5.

3. "PMS Relief," *Better Homes & Gardens*, http://www.findarticles.com/m1041/4_78/61184824/p1/article.jhtml.

4. Carol Wiley Lorente, "New Hope for PMS," *Vegetarian Times*, March 1, 1998, http://www.findarticles.com/m0820/n247/20380025/p1/article.jhtml.

Chapter 11

1. Craig A. Hill, "Gender, Relationship Stage, and Sexual Behavior: The Importance of Partner Emotional Investment with Specific Situations," *Journal of Sex Research* 39, no.3 (August 1, 2002): 22.

2. Avert, "Sexually Transmitted Diseases and STD Symptoms," http://www.avert.org/stds.htm.

3. Henry Cloud and John Townsend, *Boundaries in Dating* (Grand Rapids: Zondervan, 2000), 244–45.

4. O. Gunturkun, O, "Human Behavior: Adult Persistence of Headturning Asymmetry," *Nature* 421, no. 6924:711.

5. C.E. Weber, "Cortisol's Purpose," *Medical Hypotheses* 51 (1998): 289–92.

Chapter 13

1. E. K. Miller and J. D. Cohen, "Integrative Theory of Prefrontal Cortex Function," *Annual Review of Neuroscience* 24 (2001) 167–202, http://arjournals.annualreviews.org/doi/abs/10.1146%2Fannurev.neuro.24.1.167.

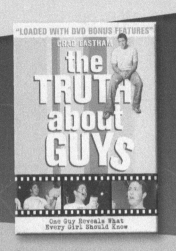
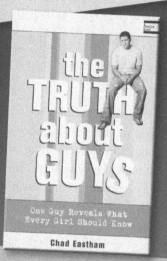

Celebrate Your Differences

Men and women know they're different, but what can they do about it? In this refreshing and humorous look at relationships, Bill and Pam Farrel explain why a man is like a waffle (each element of his life is in a separate box), why a woman is like a plate of spaghetti (everything in her life touches everything else), and how the differences can work for you.

Men Are Like Waffles—Women Are Like Spaghetti will shine a light into the marvel and mystery of the one you live with, love, and care for.

250,000 in Print

Men Are Like Waffles, Women Are Like Spaghetti

Understanding and Delighting in Your Differences

Bill and Pam Farrel

Bill and Pam Farrel are cofounders and codirectors of Masterful Living, an organization that provides practical insights for perso relationships. The Farrels are also regular relationship columnist As coauthors their books include *Men Are Like Waffles—Women Are Like Spaghetti*, *Red-Hot Monogamy*, and *The 10 Best Decision Every Couple Can Make*. The Farrels have been married nearly 3 years and have three children and a daughter-in-law.

HARVEST HOUSE PUBLISHERS

To read a sample chapter, v
www.HarvestHousePublishers.